Reimaging Africa

Adeyinka Adewale · Stefan Schepers

Reimaging Africa

Lifting the Veil of Ignorance

Adeyinka Adewale
Henley Business School
University of Reading
Reading, UK

Stefan Schepers
Henley Business School
University of Reading
Reading, UK

ISBN 978-3-031-40359-0   ISBN 978-3-031-40360-6 (eBook)
https://doi.org/10.1007/978-3-031-40360-6

© The Editor(s) (if applicable) and The Author(s), under exclusive license to Springer Nature Switzerland AG 2023

This work is subject to copyright. All rights are solely and exclusively licensed by the Publisher, whether the whole or part of the material is concerned, specifically the rights of translation, reprinting, reuse of illustrations, recitation, broadcasting, reproduction on microfilms or in any other physical way, and transmission or information storage and retrieval, electronic adaptation, computer software, or by similar or dissimilar methodology now known or hereafter developed.

The use of general descriptive names, registered names, trademarks, service marks, etc. in this publication does not imply, even in the absence of a specific statement, that such names are exempt from the relevant protective laws and regulations and therefore free for general use.

The publisher, the authors, and the editors are safe to assume that the advice and information in this book are believed to be true and accurate at the date of publication. Neither the publisher nor the authors or the editors give a warranty, expressed or implied, with respect to the material contained herein or for any errors or omissions that may have been made. The publisher remains neutral with regard to jurisdictional claims in published maps and institutional affiliations.

Cover illustration: © Melisa Hasan

This Palgrave Macmillan imprint is published by the registered company Springer Nature Switzerland AG
The registered company address is: Gewerbestrasse 11, 6330 Cham, Switzerland

Paper in this product is recyclable.

In loving memory of my father, John Babatunde Adewale, who taught me to see the world differently

Adeyinka Adewale

In memory of my mother, Germaine Lijnen who shared her love of Africans with me

Stefan Schepers

Preface

The age of iron is over, The age of magic has begun,
Unveil your years
—Ben Okri

This book is intended for people who are interested, maybe fascinated, by Africa, who have not much time to spend, but who feel a need to extend and deepen their knowledge beyond the superficialities and distortions of the remnants of colonial history telling and its continuing influence. The narrative of European domination in Africa lingers on, often unconsciously, in too many minds and hinders fair and equitable relationships today.

Nowhere is this clearer than in the idea that Europe needs to 'develop' Africa, which is nothing else than the colonial concept of 'civilising' it, cloaked in a new version, with a hint of guilt. This prevents a fresh, objective, non-European and non-Western look at Africa. Indeed, it would be useful to set narratives right for the whole world; Europe's relative amnesia for its past exploits outside the continent is not shared elsewhere. The Chinese speak, not without reason, of a century of humiliation. What has been called 'Occidentalism' and 'Eurocentrism', seeing the world from an exclusive Western perspective, is a serious obstacle on the road to more equality in today's world and is a source of much resentment by people who in fact would like to emulate the quality of life in Western societies, while preserving their own cultures. No doubt the colonising countries stand first in the line of responsibility, but all others directly and indirectly benefited and all others bought into their justification stories.

However, Africans themselves continue to ignore their own histories, outside small circles of experts, and when there was occasional public reaction to one-sided storytelling, it was mostly narrow and emotional instead of inclusive and knowledge based. Europeans meanwhile remain at risk of judging a shared history through a keyhole. There was fierce African resistance against the military invaders; and there were enlightened Europeans who did not adhere to the official narratives of imperialism, alongside well-intentioned idealists who could not grasp how they were incorporated in systemic exploitation.

How could such ignorance persist, in both continents? Africans and Europeans were rather cosmopolitan in their world views until the eighteenth century and dealt with each other in a more or less equal manner. Africans moved into European society as traders and diplomats, not just as servants and more than one prominent European had also African ancestry, now ignored. This changed when the early industrialisation in Western Europe and the development of the plantation economy in the Americas led to the search for material and human resources and for markets, and they found them plentiful in Africa. Developments in the world have never been synchronic and just like Europe benefited from a temporary cycle of stagnation in Asia, so Africa suffered from a simultaneous period of political and economic weakness. Emulating the conquest of the Americas and the massive transfer of wealth which its exploitation had brought, Africa was the next prey of European imperialism driven by economic interests. It was intellectually based now on the dominant nationalist ideology of the times, leaving little space for alternative opinions. One can regret past events from today's perspective, but one can understand them properly only within the contextual conditions and mindsets of the times when they happened.

The ruthless destruction of the resistance by African kingdoms would have wide-ranging consequences till today. They continue to shape the future of African countries, but they are still not fully recognised. One result is that Europe, despite the continuing economic intertwining, does not still take fully into account Africa's own pathway towards a free trade area (its Agenda 2063), nor the extra-territorial impact of many of its policies. The post-colonial relations smacks often of neo-colonial one, even if it is not always intentional and a result of the negligence of the historic legacy.

Historic facts show that African societies were never so conservative that they would not have developed a modern industrial economy anyway. Leading philosophers, such as Avishai Margalit and others, have often remarked that a shared memory has the power to link different societies. Memory is always multiple, and common memory can serve as an alternative to dividing forces and can have a binding role to jointly work on a better future. What is needed today is a balanced recognition of the past as a start for a new cosmopolitanism, a world view of equal respect for different histories and for different pathways to economic and social modernity.

This book hopes to make a modest contribution to opening hearts and minds. It is an essay, not a study book, though it is based on well-known existing research by top scholars, undisputed facts and serious analysis. Unfortunately, books of this nature do not reach a wide audience and are sometimes written in technical language. Therefore we have attempted to present Africa in an accessible language. We have not cluttered the book with references, but at the end, we list the works consulted as well as some further reading for those whose curiosity requires more.

The authors have each a close connection to both continents—one born in Africa but living and working in Europe for many years, the other born in Europe but professionally often in Africa, with both being friends as well as colleagues at the same business school. This background explains their focus on the Europe-Africa relationship, which is also the one most needed to be corrected, rather than on the equally ancient relationships between Africa and the Americas or Asia.

In an increasingly globalised world, the authors believe that the richness of the many ancient and diverse civilisations in Africa can offer a solid basis for a new mutually fair and equitable collaboration between them and other countries especially those of Europe given the historic Europe-Africa interactions. But the general public on both continents is only vaguely aware of much of this richness, even those who have personal experiences of the other and think of themselves as enlightened. For those, we have written this book. We kept it short and easy, so that it can be read on the long haul flights between Africa and Europe.

The preparatory research work benefited from the support of the Sawaris Foundation from Egypt and the King Baudouin Foundation from Belgium. We are grateful to both for helping to launch this initiative. At the start, we benefited also from the insights of Gerald Abila, Geert Laporte, Rabad El Mahdi, Mohammed Marm Salih, Jacqueline Musiitwa,

Njeri Mwagiru and Rainer Thiele. Gratitude goes to them too. We were supported by Oladiran Oladosu during the research phase, and by John Maré during the drafting phase, while Patricia Waller-Hogg brought us linguistic expertise. All opinions and potential weaknesses remain our own responsibility.

The idea of this book was initiated during discussions in a Brussels public-private sector think tank, the independent High-Level Group on Africa-Europe Partnership, at the time of preparations for the African-European Summit in February 2022, whose meagre results proved again how much remains to be done.

We dedicate the book to Leopold Senghor, the philosopher, poet and statesman, perhaps the first African at the end of colonialism to show the inclusiveness of the values of both civilisations.

Reading, UK
Adeyinka Adewale
Stefan Schepers

Contents

1	**Introduction**	1
	A Veil of Ignorance	1
2	**Pre-colonial Political Order in Africa**	9
	Introduction	9
	Egypt and North African Kingdoms	10
	The Sahel and West African Kingdoms and Empires	15
	Central African Kingdoms and Empires	22
	Southern African Kingdoms and Empires	24
	East African Kingdoms and Empires	29
	Conclusion	35
3	**Pillars of Africa's Ancient Economies**	39
	Introduction	39
	Economic Structures in Pre-Colonial Africa	40
	Economic Activities in Pre-Colonial Africa	42
	Crops, Livestock and Fish	42
	Manufacturing	44
	Mining	46
	Currencies in Pre-Colonial Africa	47
	Going Global	54
	The Economic Decline of Pre-Colonial Africa	62

4	**African Pre-Colonial Social and Political Structures**	67
	Introduction	67
	Communitarianism as a Basis for African Social Values	69
	Families and Clans as Basic Units of African Societies	71
	From Clans to City-States: The Evolution of African Societies	73
	African Pre-Colonial Socio-Political Structures and Systems	76
	Colonisation and African Socio-Political Structures	82
	Implications for African Values Systems	85
	Conclusions	87
5	**Colonialism and the Struggle for Independence**	91
	Introduction: The Twilight of the Colonial Period	91
	African Nationalism in the Struggle for Independence	93
	Colonial Oppression	95
	Missionary Churches and Education	96
	World Wars I and II	99
	Europe's Golden Age of Economic Growth	100
	African Post-Colonial Independence	107
6	**An Interdependency Stuck in the Past**	115
	The Original Sin	118
	The Long Twilight of Colonialism	122
	Reparation of the Minds	129
	Forging a Constructive Interdependence	130
	Creating a Virtuous Cycle	137
7	**Facing the Future**	141
Bibliography		155
Index		169

CHAPTER 1

Introduction

A Veil of Ignorance

In the majestic landscapes of Africa, a grand history has played out. Kingdoms and empires have risen and vanished, industrious people enjoyed welfare comparable to elsewhere, trade links crisscrossed the continent, war and peace alternated, a humanistic philosophy enriched hearts and minds, and arts flourished. A truly unique civilisation, rich and diverse, covered by a veil of ignorance.

From Egypt it influenced ancient Greece, Europe's own civilisation has African roots. However, in contemporary Europe, knowledge of history has declined, mental gaps abound, a source of many frictions and of short-sightedness. In European mindsets, this ignorance is a source of condescendence and hubris; in African mindsets, it leads to feelings of humiliation and victimisation. Self-flagellation or hysteria thrive on cognitive gaps, unfortunately, they are spreading nowadays just when we are in dire need of cool minds. This all hinders the design of common, though not identical, pathways to future welfare for the people, at a time when global challenges make this more important than ever.

The first step towards better interhuman relations is always a recognition of evidence, however unpleasant it may be, and to put away distorting, incomplete narratives. The second is to foster mutual understanding, not just of facts and figures, but of the deeper historic, cultural and social realities which influence people's frame of mind. People who

© The Author(s), under exclusive license to Springer Nature
Switzerland AG 2023
A. Adewale and S. Schepers, *Reimaging Africa*,
https://doi.org/10.1007/978-3-031-40360-6_1

live today have no responsibility for what happened then, but they do for remedying the remaining consequences.

The seventeenth–eighteenth century Age of Enlightenment brought science and rationalism to the forefront of thinking, and this led to unique humanistic progress. People in the so-called West, the first part of the world to put it into practice, lead longer and healthier lives, with more material comforts and security than ever before in history. On every criterium of a happy life, today's people are better of, though the consumerist culture can be spiritually quite empty and individualism can ignore the importance of the commons. However, no one in Africa or elsewhere would like to return to the mortality rates of the past, to name but one issue on the list of progress.

However, history's balance sheet has two sides. It is often politically expedient to overlook this. Westerners like to be proud of their quality of life, and with good reason. But while nearly every refugee in the world likes to reach a Western country, the global system created by the West does not correspond to the Enlightenment ideals applied at home, not without struggle there either. Africans know this well, given the continuing legacy of European imperialism, though this period, in particular the later part of the twentieth century, also left some Enlightenment benefits.

History is always written by the winners of military or economic wars. The latter are less visibly brutal, but unfair trade by an economically dominant power is no less destructive of other societies in the long term. To justify such exploitative relationships, victors manipulate not only current evidence, but they also rewrite the political, economic, social and cultural past of the countries subjugated. They seek to control people's minds here and there, about their past and their future.

Since the beginning of European imperialism in the fifteenth century and in particular in the nineteenth century, European countries have practised this in Africa and elsewhere in the world, though not all in equal measure; later the United States would become the dominant economic and military force following European footsteps. The industrialisation and the growth of economically powerful West would not have been possible to the same extent and in the same, historically speaking, a short term without military dominance and diverse forms of economic and social exploitation of other countries. This dominance may have become more hidden, but the global institutional setup dating from the post-Second World War period has not yet been adapted to new contextual conditions and the current ecological and economic needs of mankind. The cosmopolitanism of the ancient, pre-colonial world is still a distant project, though without it there is likely to be a global disaster, if only because of excessive inequality, in many (dis)guises. As the French writer Emile Zola famously warned in the nineteenth century 'The rich will understand the social question in front of their burning villas'. Imperial conquest is familiar to all continents in history, driven by economic interests sometimes coupled with religion and ideology, but the current predicaments of the world indicate the need for cosmopolitanism and global institutional collaboration. New technologies, if used for the common benefit, may make it possible.

It usually takes three generations for historic developments to fade out of living memory, but they can linger on much longer in subconscious collective memories, percolating through the generations by the combined effects of education and religion. To these one can add today the role of both the established media and the new communication means.

African societies are designing their own pathway to economic and social modernity, which should bring them to welfare and security in life. But it is impossible without looking back at the contextual realities surviving after nearly two centuries of dominance and exploitation by outside powers. The wealth of and the relations between countries in Africa were broadly speaking comparable to the rest of the world, before Europe's industrialisation allowed it to economically and politically overtake all other countries, including Japan, India or China. These had been more advanced than Europe before, using the yardsticks designed by Europeans for the rest of the world. Contrary to the usual narrative, it is becoming evident nowadays that colonisation distorted Africa's own indigenous path towards industrial modernisation, by forcing it to serve European economic interests, despite some beneficiation.

Many leading economists today have shown that the relatively rapid industrialisation in Europe would not have been possible in the same way without internal labour exploitation and external resource extraction, hence the colonial wars waged by European powers against the rest of the world in the same period. The exploitation of labour has gradually been reduced through the building of unique welfare state systems in Europe, though not without struggle. Some of this trickled down in the colonies. But the economic and trade imbalances still needs to be fundamentally remedied through systemic changes. In practice, Europe, and the West in general, often do the opposite of what they preach. Even when they try to help, they do so from their perspective instead of the local one.

People are not responsible for the opinions and actions of their ancestors. This is an intellectual and moral aberration. But people today are surely responsible for the lasting impact, and even more for current neocolonial policies, when they are dealing with the global challenges today, in the first place climate change and inequality which are partly related. Climate change affects everyone everywhere. This should be a stimulus to build a fairer world led by shared humanistic ideals and common interest. European countries, at war for centuries, have shown through the process of building a Union that it can be done, indeed that it is necessary given the evolution of technologies and the increase of economic interdependencies and their societal impact. African countries, through their Union, albeit institutionally much looser and politically far more prudent, and thus slow with structural reforms, seem intend to seek a comparable way towards peace and economic growth.

However, this will not be possible without a change of mindsets. Until the end of the eighteenth century, GDP was broadly comparable in the known world. Then, Western growth raced forward and they could no longer keep up with its industrialisation, science and technology, and capital markets. The West's superiority complex is based on these material successes, which brought more welfare than ever before in history. But this is not enough justification for such a mentality, unless perhaps for people who believe that social life is limited to economic or monetary statistics. However, one cannot ignore either that Africa's current conditions are not only a result of this past and that some are self-made, as Moeletsi Mbeki, among others, has shown in his remarkable book 'Architects of poverty'.

We must strive towards a new cosmopolitanism, based on plural identities, as existed before the age of European conquest of other countries, without which it will be probably impossible to deal with the global challenges today. We need to discard the identity politics of the past, based on the Westphalian nation-state concept and a singular definition of people's identity, and well as the new identity politics which equally divide people instead of bringing them together. It is in everybody's interest to take a more dispassionate view of social organisation and the modern state system.

Political order emerges in history in relation mainly to economic conditions of people. Hunters and gatherers had a different need for order in their small, continuously trekking societies than early settled farming communities, as shown in the great fertile deltas of the Nile and elsewhere. Order in feudal agricultural societies aimed at ensuring food production and distribution. An increase of population, trade or external threats led to more centralised political order, while industrialisation made the more complex state of today a necessity.

While Europeans are usually familiar with their own developments of political order, albeit often a constructed view to serve temporary interests, from Roman times till modern state formation and beyond, they also knew about different political order in faraway countries which they traded with. There was much curiosity about them, sometimes admiration about the magnificence of their courts—they knew how they had bow for the Emperor of China or the King of the Kongo—sometimes also justified revulsion about certain practices—widows dying with their husbands in India, for example.

Before the emergence of the modern state in Europe, after the religious wars were ended by the Westphalian Peace Treaty in 1648, political order was not fundamentally different in Africa or Europe. Predominantly agricultural societies were ruled by an aristocratic class with a king or emperor at the head, with a small administration for markets and trade; bonded labour existed in different forms everywhere. Social norms were enforced through religious practices. There were various kinds of redistribution systems to ensure social coherence and stability. All this was known by traders and reported, mostly in an anecdotal way.

It is therefore all the more surprising that the notion that Africa had no history became the prevalent concept of the 'dark continent' in the nineteenth and twentieth centuries. It has, no doubt, shaped the relationship between Westerners and Africans until the twenty-first century. The history of Africa, even for many Africans, has been substantially reduced to one tragic aspect, the exportation of African slaves to the Americas (the equally large slave trade to Arab countries and Asia is ignored, because only men were taken there and they were prevented from having offspring, and the slavery of large numbers of Europeans is equally not mentioned). For many, this has become now 'the' history of Europeans in Africa, and it is as reductionist as the colonial view was. Moreover, it is overlooked that colonies and colonial power differed greatly from country to country.

Despite the historical realities of a continuous interface, albeit with variable intensity, between Europe and Africa, the narrow notions of

Africa persisted and permeated European perceptions of Africa. Such an unjustified paradigm has helped strengthen European views that Africa did not have much of a history or societal structures before the era of European colonisation. This probably helped stoke European feelings of superiority, often used as justification for historical European imperialism and exploitation in Africa, and elsewhere. It is repeated nowadays by the North Americans.

What the Greeks referred to as Ethiopia was, in essence, the ancient kingdom of Kush in the broader region of Nubia, stretching from the present-day southern edge of Egypt to the place where the White and Blue Niles meet at Khartoum in what is now southern Sudan. The Nubians were renowned for their complex societies and states, including Kerma, the capital city of the Kerma culture, which for the ancient Egyptians became synonymous with the Kingdom of Kush and was renowned for its particularly vibrant economy, culture and military skills.

North Africa has always been more involved with Europe. Geography certainly played a major role in this. However, North Africa also had classical civilisations and development more akin to those in Europe. Furthermore, it was generally not perceived in the same manner by Europeans as the societies of sub-Saharan Africa, despite sharing a colonial era with European control for many years. European control of sub-Saharan Africa generally occurred in the nineteenth century based on earlier trade patterns, whereas North African colonisation and control by Europeans followed a different trajectory.

In recent times, Europe's 'development' activities in Africa became a key theme of, and often helped further strengthen, the unequal state of the relationship. This development paradigm has frequently masked the civilisational one from the nineteenth century used to justify economic imperialism, sometimes still coupled with military interventions.

In the early twentieth century, in the late years of the colonial era, many Europeans developed a new interest in and theories about both the nature of African societies and how they differ from European-type cultures and societies. By then, the latter were generally referred to as 'modern', or 'Western', given that they were led by the countries of Western Europe. Subsequently 'developed' and 'underdeveloped' grew increasingly into rigid paradigms, framing and influencing the actions and relationships of stakeholders within them. There was hardly any appreciation for non-European values and standards. This process further strengthened European condescendence for much of Africa, whose societies with cultures much different from those of Europe were locked into an inferior position, politically and economically, vis-à-vis their European rulers.

Nevertheless, from the end of the nineteenth century onwards, there were enlightened, critical, divergent views too. One of the first Europeans who made a major contribution to new consideration being given to African societies was the German ethnologist Leo Frobenius. His work helped focus new attention on African societies as being both different from Europeans yet having substance worthy of understanding with respect. The new interest in African cultures resulting from the work of Frobenius and others and by him taking African art to Europe for exhibitions, led to African traditional legends and storytelling being brought to the attention of the European public for the first time.

In Africa, one of the foremost African thinkers and writers whose work has had considerable relevance in promoting a new regard for things African in Europe was Léopold Senghor. He was not only the first President of post-colonial, independent Senegal but also a key founder of the 'Négritude' school of thought. He once claimed that it was Frobenius who had 'given Africa back its dignity and identity'. Négritude was one of the first major intellectual movements of Africans resident in Africa and in the African diaspora, aimed at raising and cultivating 'Black consciousness'.

It was initially intended for Africa, but had a broad international impact, especially in French-speaking cultures and intellectual circles. It illustrated initial moves towards cultural cross-pollination from the Europe-Africa interface and this happened most clearly in the arts. The influence of Africa in the early twentieth century was very significant in the course of modern visual arts, music or literature in the West. True it would take almost a century still until African art itself would move out of the ethnographic categorisation and accepted as great art on its own merits (such as in the new Museum at the Quai Branly in Paris).

The book starts with a bird's eye overview of the principal political organisations, the kingdoms and empires in Africa since about the beginning of our calendar, though Egypt is the oldest known and grandest civilisation on the African continent long before, and one with a clear influence on the developments in the eastern Mediterranean, ancient Greece and Rome.

Political order always and everywhere is a function of economic structures, in the first place the production and provision of food to the people, but also of the tools and amenities of life, as well as luxuries and objects of beauty and significance for religious and political ceremonies. This is briefly presented in the second chapter.

Political and economic structures rest also on metaphysical concepts, on a collective view of social interaction, on ethics and family life, on the role of authority and consensus building, what European call democracy.

In the next chapter, we examine how African societies rose up again, after the initial knockdown of colonialism, and launched independence movements, in fact, an unforeseen by-product of the ideas which Europeans spread themselves through the newly established education systems, and of the enlisting of African soldiers for their own wars.

In the last chapters, the ups and downs of the contemporary relationship between Africa and Europe are examined, with a focus on the role of the European Union, the collective new political and economic order of most European countries.

Inspired by research and analysis of many people and study centres, also by the discussions in the independent High-Level Group on Africa-Europe Partnership, we conclude by sharing our views on concrete steps towards a fair and equitable new relationship, which must be built bottom-up, engaging civic societies and business. This is the task for a generation of young people on both continents, in their own mutual interest.

CHAPTER 2

Pre-colonial Political Order in Africa

INTRODUCTION

Egypt was probably the prime mover of Africa's interaction with the outside world through an interconnected web of regional and international trade routes dating back millennia BC. Trade routes between Thebes and the Red Sea ports connected northern Africa to Asia, Arabia and East Africa through the Horn of Africa. At the same time, trade spanned the north-eastern corner of the Sahara, connecting Egypt to Nubia, the Libyan Desert, the cultures of the eastern Mediterranean and Senegal (West Africa). These were linked to trade routes deeper into the continent. Through the extensive connections in this trans-Saharan route, Africans traded and transported gold, silver, ivory, obsidian, salt, spices, animals, iron, wheat and other plants.

Controlling these routes was important to trade supremacy which always brings a premium. For example, the Greek expansion (by Alexander the Great) into Egypt in 322 BC helped Greece gain a major foothold along the spice route and access to India and China. Rome, after supplanting Greece in 146 BC and taking Egypt in 31 BC, would go on to solidify, fortify and extend its north African trade links and in the process firmly connect other societies in the Sahel and West Africa that had established themselves as important stops along the trans-Saharan trade route. The trade links across the Sahara were further strengthened after the Muslim conquest of North Africa (between 647 and 709

© The Author(s), under exclusive license to Springer Nature Switzerland AG 2023
A. Adewale and S. Schepers, *Reimaging Africa*,
https://doi.org/10.1007/978-3-031-40360-6_2

AD) and the introduction of the camel to the trans-Saharan route. The camel caravans were one of the greatest logistical achievements ever, only surpassed many centuries later by road and rail transport.

As often happened, societies connected by these trade routes eventually formed the foundations of major empires and kingdoms which were particularly suited to driving the trade relationships. This was especially the case for the Sahel and West Africa, yet was also a major feature elsewhere in Africa, and in particular on the Eastern shores with India and China. In the course of history, Europe's role as an economic and trading partner has remained of special significance for Africa, though differing over the centuries.

The countries of the southern Mediterranean naturally had the closest link with them, and their influence on Europe's future development was significant, in particular, that of Egypt and later Carthage.

Egypt and North African Kingdoms

Egypt especially had a reputation not just as a Biblical realm, but also as a cradle of civilisation. Its pyramids, hieroglyphs and tombs for the pharaohs had long fascinated European philosophers and historians. In ancient times, other empires apart from Egypt of special relevance in the north of the continent were those of Kush and Carthage.

The whole region to the south of Egypt known as Nubia had seen many sophisticated and economically complex societies focussed on agriculture and trade. From the earliest times, the Egyptians had identified Kerma, the capital, as 'Kush' and for a number of centuries, the two civilisations had a close relationship which included intermittent warfare as well as trade and cultural exchanges. In 1504 BC Egypt annexed Nubia and by 1500 BC had absorbed it into the New Kingdom of Egypt, a considerable gain for the New Kingdom which nevertheless disintegrated afterwards in about 1075 BC. Shortly thereafter in around 1070 BC, Kush re-emerged as an independent kingdom.

Kush would go on to become an important regional power amongst other things invading and ruling as the 25th Dynasty of Egypt, known as the dynasty of the Black Pharaohs. The kingdom also engaged in battles against Assyria (677 BC) and Roman Egypt (23 BC) and despite some defeats lasted for about 300 years. Alongside their solid military, the Kushites had a vibrant economy. They traded in ivory, incense, gold and iron. Interestingly, they were able to simultaneously trade with and wage war against Egypt.

The kingdom of Punt (in the Horn of Africa) was both a significant trading partner and a source of cultural and religious influence for the Egyptians. It is believed that trade with Egypt began as early as the reign of Pharaoh Khufu in the 4th Dynasty of Egypt (2613–1983 BC) and probably even earlier. It has been historically verified that an expedition was made to it during the reign of the Egyptian Pharaoh Pepi II Neferkare around 2200 BC. Voyages were furthermore undertaken during the 11th Dynasty of Egypt (2081–1938 BC) which resulted in the first successful attempt known at transplanting foreign plants. Punt was also known for producing and exporting gold, aromatic resins, blackwood, ebony, ivory and wild animals just as it opened up to the Greeks following Alexander the Great's conquest of Egypt.

The other empire of special relevance in ancient North Africa was Carthage which at its height was one of the largest, richest and most influential in the world. The Carthaginian Empire was a conglomeration of independent Phoenician city-states located in North Africa and modern Spain (575 BC to 146 BC), that was controlled by the city-state of Carthage (in present-day Tunisia).

From a minor port on the coast where Phoenician traders stopped to resupply or repair their ships, it grew into a major centre of trade. Carthage's growth was significantly facilitated by the fall of Tyre to Alexander the Great in 332 BC, whose refugees greatly helped the empire's growth. It was also facilitated by the numerous colonies, vassals, satellite states and trading posts it established along the coasts of the Mediterranean. Colonies were established in North Africa and Iberia such that by 300 BC, they controlled the largest part of the region. Recent research has shown trade links across the Sahara with the interior of Africa.

It is interesting to note how perceptions can change. Arabs considered northern Africa, Barbary, as an island, surrounded by water and desert. The Sahara itself was an obstacle, never a barrier to trade and the establishment of Phoenician trade posts and the growth of Carthage doubtless stimulated trans-Sahara trade.

Motives for setting up trading posts, an embryonic step of colonisation, then and later, were usually for practical economic and political motives to enhance trade without outside interference. When trade became threatened, military intervention could follow quickly. All of this led Carthage to increase its wealth and influence. The Greeks followed a similar strategy of establishing colonies across the Mediterranean and the Black Sea and became a competing maritime power. Just like the site chosen to found Carthage, the Phoenicians strategically selected the locations of their colonies with great care, focussing on the quality of harbours and their proximity to trade routes.

From its advantageous location, Carthage not only controlled the sea traffic with its colonies but also extended its influence by land across the Sahara. Carthage's ships visited every major port of the Mediterranean and the Atlantic coasts of Africa sometimes carrying over 100 tonnes of goods. Archaeological evidence shows the exchange of all manner of goods including tin (needed for bronze-based civilisations), textiles, ceramics, fine metalwork, silver, lead, copper and purple dye. The purple dye became one of the most highly valued commodities in the ancient Mediterranean, being worth fifteen to twenty times its weight in gold.

In addition to its extensive trade network, Carthage's location also helped it increase its wealth through agriculture, for instance through the trading of salted Atlantic fish and manufacturing. It was well known for its embroidered silks, cotton, linen, wool, pottery, faience, incense and perfumes. Other exotic goods and household items such as jewellery, arts and furniture, were created from ivory, glassware, wood, alabaster, bronze, brass, lead, gold and silver. On land, Carthage sent caravans into the interior of Africa and Persia and traded its manufactured and agricultural produce for precious stones and animals through auctions, invented by its merchants and deployed widely for trade with African kingdoms. In addition to its lucrative business in maritime trade, it increased wealth through tribute and tariffs.

The empire's navy was one of the largest and most powerful in the ancient Mediterranean. The navy helped facilitate Carthage's economic rise by protecting and securing its trade interests across various sea routes. This helped it enforce trade monopolies against competitors while also levering its fleets for exploring and finding new trade routes or markets. Except for its predominantly Punic navy, Carthage relied heavily on foreign mercenaries, including those from Europe, and multi-ethnic alliances. Carthage leveraged its vast wealth and hegemony to make up its army ranks by maintaining close relations, sometimes through political marriages, with the rulers of various tribes and kingdoms.

It was this expansion, especially into Sicily, that brought Carthage into conflict first with the Greeks (between 580 and 265 BC), and then with Rome (between 264 and 146 BC). By 310 BC, Carthage controlled almost all of Sicily and laid siege to Syracuse itself. It then engaged in a series of historic battles against Rome that had become emboldened by its expansion into the colonies of Magna Graecia, increasing its domination of the Italian peninsula. Over the course of the next century, two subsequent major conflicts that would determine the course of Western civilisation ensued between Rome and Carthage, one of which nearly prevented the rise of the Roman Empire.

In the second Punic War, Hannibal went on to win a series of decisive battles against the Romans including one at Lake Trasimeno where his troops all but annihilated the Roman army. Not until the Zulus defeated the British and the Ethiopians the Italians in the nineteenth century, would the African military achieve such a victory over Europeans. Nevertheless, after years of costly fighting that brought both empires to the verge of destruction, the Romans managed to achieve the final victory, imposing harsh and retributive peace conditions on Carthage. Though the third Punic War was the smallest, it was to be the most decisive resulting in the destruction of the city of Carthage, where city population of a million inhabitants had fifty thousand remaining at final surrender. The survivors were sold into slavery, the city was razed, and the territory was made a Roman province under the name of Africa, which it remained until it was captured by the Arabs in 705 AD.

It is important to note that the key to Carthage's significance for global civilisational development was its ability to adapt as an empire to foster its growth and expansion. For example, although the Carthaginians retained the traditional Phoenician affinity for maritime trade and commerce, it was their imperial and military ambitions that distinguished them.

Although an oligarchic republic, it benefited from an intricate system of checks and balances, a complex administrative system, civil society and a fairly high degree of public accountability and participation. At its head were two non-hereditary judges (called Sufetes) who had judicial and executive power and were elected annually from among the most influential families. The mandates within which the Sufetes could exercise their powers were quite similar to those of present-day presidents in parliamentary republics, in that their power wasn't absolute and was for the most part exercised in ceremonial functions. Most of the political power rested in a supreme council (or council of elders) of thirty elected members who controlled the wealth of the state. Besides the supreme council, there was a judicial tribunal called the One Hundred and Four, which was some sort of supreme court in today's terms. They have a primary function to oversee the administration of law across different strata of society and government in the interest of the republic.

As part of the Roman Empire, North Africa was of great importance to Rome, because it was the breadbasket of the Roman Empire. A network of major Roman cities along this coastline and its hinterland were important among other things as trading and military outposts vis-a-vis the West African nations on the other side of the Sahara. With Rome's expansion into North Africa, the whole continent became more firmly linked to the global trade system through the trans-Saharan routes with Egypt at the centre. Rome's impact was such that when the empire crumbled in the fifth century AD, the prosperity of the nations under its influence began to unravel, first in Europe and later, in Africa. With the Islamic expansion into North Africa, Western Europe lost the centrepiece around which it had structured its prosperity: access to trade. Eastern Europe, Byzantium, however, maintained access to the east through the capital of the Eastern Roman Empire, Constantinople.

Following the conquest of North Africa by the Islamic armies in the seventh century AD, the region was again of major relevance as a cultural, religious and economic bridge but now between Africa and the broader, Islamic Middle East/Mediterranean regions. This was followed by the establishment of the Ottoman Empire with its capital at Constantinople which saw it become not only an empire with great influence in the international context but also an important player in Africa which its conquest of Egypt in 1517 especially helped to deliver.

After the conquest of Constantinople by the Ottoman Turks, the importance and influence of both the Ottoman Empire and Ottoman Egypt, if one were to regard them as two entities, on East as well as North Africa remained considerable. Although in the nineteenth century, Egypt had secured great autonomy from its nominal Ottoman rulers in Constantinople, in reality being under British occupation in the post-Napoleonic era, it actually interacted with Constantinople as well as Europe and down the Nile Valley into East Africa as an African state rather than on behalf of the Ottoman Empire.

The position of the Ottoman Empire in North Africa gradually diminished in the late nineteenth and early twentieth centuries, primarily because of the increased British military interventions in Egypt and of France along the rest of the North African littoral. The French presence was of particular importance as a bridge between France and indeed Europe on the one hand and both North Africa and to a lesser extent

Africa, on the other. In all this, the region of North Africa continued to play a major role in the Africa-Europe relationship. During the period of European colonialism, there was a particularly nuanced tone in many ways, possibly with a greater respectful acknowledgement of the other side than was the case in many other parts of Africa. Yet, with increased exploitation and military oppression, it experienced similar resentment and struggles for independence as the rest of African colonial situations.

The Sahel and West African Kingdoms and Empires

The Ghana Empire (not to be confused with modern-day Ghana), commonly known as Wagadu, was probably the first of the major empires to be established in the region and it existed around 700–1240 AD. It comprised complex societies in the present-day region of Mauritania, Senegal and Mali. The empire specialised in and grew significantly rich from trading in gold, salt and kola nuts, which allowed for the development of large urban centres in the region. The first to benefit from the introduction of gold mining, Ghana dominated other smaller states in the region for centuries and the increased trade in gold and salt enabled its territorial expansion to control different trade routes.

Its dominant position was lost to the Mali Empire after the Almoravids (a Muslim empire centred in Morocco between 1040 and 1147 BC) invaded Ghana in 1076 BC. The rise of the Mali Empire in 1240 AD eventually sealed its collapse when it was incorporated as a vassal state within the Empire of Mali, one of several great economically and culturally important early states in African history.

Around 1235 BC, King Sundaita Keita founded the Mali Empire by uniting several smaller kingdoms near the Upper Niger River that were revolting against trade restrictions placed on them by the king of Ghana, Sumanguru. Over the course of four centuries, by using its well-trained imperial army, Mali was able to conquer more territories and extend its influence and culture throughout the region. Its expansion strengthened its control of trade routes and coupled with its significant gold and copper resources it grew to become one of the wealthiest empires ever.

Its founder, Keita is rightly renowned for creating one of the very first charters of human rights—the Manden Charter (or the Kouroukan Fouga), about the same time as several European counterparts, the beginning of the modern rule of law. Though not a written charter, it has been handed down orally through generations and advocates peace in diversity, the inviolability of the human being, education, the integrity of the motherland, food security, the abolition of slavery by raids and freedom of expression and trade.

The Mali Empire enjoyed its golden age under the rulership of Mansa Musa, whom many consider to be its most influential ruler. A devout Muslim, on his way to hajj in Mecca, his caravan gave away so much gold along the trans-Saharan trade route that it took Egypt over a decade to recover from gold inflation. However, by spreading so much gold, Mansa Musa strategically accomplished two things. Firstly, he established himself and Mali as crucial to the trans-Saharan trade. Secondly, he established a demand for Mali's gold. Arab and European explorers made their way to Timbuktu in search of Mansa's gold. Timbuktu became famous for the Sankore, a fully staffed Islamic university with one of the world's largest libraries (holding roughly 1,000,000 manuscripts) and capable of housing thousands of students.

Meanwhile, as Mali continued to expand territorially under Mansa Musa's reign, it incorporated different religious, ethnic and linguistic groups which had to be managed through provincial divisions ruled by appointed governors. These governors oversaw the administrative record, which was kept in centralised government offices at Niani as well as local taxes, justice and tribal dispute resolutions. The Malian empire continued to grow as it conquered territories and gain access to more natural resources. Besides its wealth, military strength, culture and education, Mali was also known for its architecture and art. The buildings of the Mali Empire, some of which like the Sankore mosque in Timbuktu still stand (now a UNESCO world heritage site), are one of the most famous features of the region and international symbols of Africa's rich pre-colonial history.

Despite its military strength, wealth and influence, the combination of leadership issues, mismanagement of resources, trade opportunities outside its influence, the growing trade influence and military strength of the emerging Songhai Empire and the military superiority of the Moroccan Empire would eventually lead to Mali's decline.

Trade helped the emergence of several rival kingdoms, notably the Songhai. European ships, especially Portuguese, had started sailing down regularly to the west coast of Africa. Consequently, the Saharan caravans faced ever more competition as the most efficient means to transport goods from West Africa to the Mediterranean. In the late fifteenth century, the rump of the Malian empire was incorporated into the Songhai empire. The Malian empire became reduced to controlling a small western pocket of its once great territory. In the end, Mali's success ineluctably impelled it to its decline. The empire outgrew its political and military strength, and it was unable to quell a rebellion within and outside the kingdoms it had conquered. By about 1550 AD, it had ceased to be important as a political entity while the Songhai Empire assumed now dominant control of the Sahel/Western region of Africa.

The Songhai were originally several groups of people who settled in the region of Gao from around 800 AD. Having been incorporated into the Mali Empire, Mali was unable to maintain its control of Gao during the period of its decline, paving the way for Gao to win back its independence. The Songhai would then go through about a century of vicissitudes until the 1464 AD accession of Sonni Ali who became the first king of the Songhai Empire. By 1468 AD, he was able to rid the empire of existential dangers by repulsing various attacks. He led the Songhai Empire to become one of the wealthiest and largest medieval African empires, covering the region of the present-day states of Niger, Mali, Mauritania, Senegal, Nigeria, Guinea, Gambia, southern Algeria, Burkina-Faso, Benin and Ivory Coast, surpassing the Mali Empire in area, wealth and power.

The empire's peak came during the reign of Muhammad Ture (Muhammad I Askia). He reorganised the concrete territories into provinces managed by appointed governors and extended its powers as far west as the Atlantic Ocean. He created administrative systems for the empire's finance such as the adoption of weights, measures, tithes and tax. Regulatory measures were also implemented for the empire's agriculture and fishing, justice, water and forests. With such a vast territory, the Songhai Empire was able to control multiple trading routes using camels, donkeys and boats (up and down the Niger River). On top of its already abundant supply of gold, it also controlled the salt trade. Vigorous trade policies and the use of canals for agricultural purposes also contributed to increased trade as well as the organised clan-based economy that Songhai was. Songhai was as stratified society where a person's clan ultimately decided their occupation and influence.

The Songhai system of organised labour resembled modern-day unions, with craft guilds in the empire that consisted of various mechanics and artisans. The adoption of Islam also made communication and trading in the trans-Saharan region more efficient and profitable for Songhai. It became easier for Muslims in towns within the empire to act as middlemen in the gold trade with the Akan states of West Africa. Likewise, the re-establishment of Timbuktu and Djenne as international centres of Islamic learning also contributed to the empire's grandeur.

Like Mali before it, internal strife and civil unrest started the decline of the Songhai Empire. Its greatest undoing, however, was that the empire never modernised its military. In the midst of the chaos and civil unrest, Morocco invaded Songhai in 1591 AD, amongst other likely motivations, to seize control of the trans-Saharan salt-gold trade route which gave it an important place in international trade and significant tax revenues. However, the expansion of European trade routes around the whole coast of Africa had begun to undermine the flow of gold across the desert. Also, Portugal's failed attack on Morocco in 1578 AD left Morocco on the verge of economic depletion and bankruptcy.

Another prominent kingdom in Western Africa was the Kingdom of Benin. Established by the Edo people (in present-day south-western Nigeria) in the late 1100 s AD, the kingdom was ruled by semi-mythical kings called the *Ogisos*. In its prime, through a succession of Obas (or kings) including Oba Ewuare the Great, Benin expanded its rule over the tribes of the Niger Delta, the eastern Yoruba peoples and the region currently called Lagos, all in present-day Nigeria. Benin was known, not just for its military capabilities, but also for its advanced development in architecture, art and trade. For instance, it boasted a moat around the kingdom's capital and hundreds of walls that divided it into separate, distinct areas depending on what trade would be undertaken there. This included an 11 km-long earthen rampart girded by a 20ft-deep moat that enclosed the king's palace. It created some of the world's most famous art—the Benin Bronzes, which were elaborately decorated cast plaques of commemorative heads, animals and human figures, considered artistically equal to the greatest ancient Greek art—all items of royal regalia and personal ornaments that paid tribute to Benin royalty, culture and history. Benin was also the first West African state to begin trade relations with the Portuguese, exchanging slaves and tropical products like ivory, pepper and palm oil for manillas (a form of currency used at the time) and guns. Benin continued to exist as a kingdom until it was invaded, burnt down and annexed as a British protectorate in 1897 AD.

There were other states such as the Kanem-Borno Empire and the Sokoto Caliphate which also depended on the trans-Saharan route whereas the Yorubaland, Dahomey kingdom and Akan states benefited from trade on the Atlantic. Kanem-Bornu was a predominantly trading empire that controlled the area around Lake Chad from the ninth to the nineteenth century. Initially established in 700 AD as the Kanem Empire, its territory at various times included the present-day regions of southern Chad, northern Cameroon, north-eastern Nigeria, eastern Niger and southern Libya, and played a key role in the slave trade, selling European and African slaves on its markets.

New trading partners such as the Hausa (in what is now northern Nigeria) and closer contact with the Muslim world, increased the trade of ostrich feathers and ivory. Together with diplomatic relations, a modernised army also played a big part in Kanem-Borno's expansion. The empire reached the limits of its territorial expansion between 1564 and 1596 AD, gaining control over Hausaland, among others. Diplomatic alliance with Morocco helped increase its influence on the Sahara as did the use of firearms imported from North Africa and Turkish mercenaries. The empire eventually fell as a repercussion of the Fulani War of 1804–1808 AD. Its decline was further expedited by regional particularism and attacks by the militant Wadai Empire. What was left of it was absorbed by the Northern Nigeria Protectorate in 1902, within the sphere of the British Empire.

The Sokoto Caliphate, founded in 1804 by Usman dan Fodio, who succeeded Kanem-Borno as the dominating power in the region post Fulani War. He went on to create what he hoped would be a model community of true Islam in his hometown of Degel, which as in other Islamic societies under Ulama leadership, could resist the state and its version of Islam in the name of the Sharia. Usman dan Fodio oversaw the organisation of the caliphate and its expansion, such that by the end of his different wars, the Fulanis had captured Katsina, Kano, Daura and Gobir and dan Fodio's son, Muhammed Bello, founded the city of Sokoto, which became the capital of the caliphate. The Sokoto Caliphate was developed within the context of multiple, independent Hausa kingdoms and at its height linked over thirty different emirates and had a population of over 10 million people. In the meantime, the jihad had created a new slaving frontier that about 2.5 million slaves by 1900 (second only to the American South which had four million in 1860). Slaves were gained through raiding and slave markets which depleted some of its vast regions and hampered its economic progression. Slave labour was also critical to the expansion of agricultural plantations under the caliphate.

The industry was gradually desolated in the caliphate by oppressive tax regimes. The unified political and economic Islamic movement that

Usman dan Fodio foresaw was lost. By 1903 Sokoto Caliphate was defeated and abolished by the British colonial forces and part of it was taken by the French and Germans. The honorary position of the Sultan was retained and continues to be an influential religious and political leader.

Closer to the Atlantic, there were three important kingdoms, Benin, Ife and Oyo. Ife was one of the oldest trading nations throughout the region, famous for its manufacture of glass beads and copper, and its refined architecture. They all were Yoruba-speaking people, extending their influence in parts of present-day Nigeria, Togo, Benin and Ghana. Their most dominant state was the Oyo Empire, ruled by the 'Alaafin', from 1400 till 1896, with an apogee during the seventeenth–eighteenth centuries. However, internal political conflict and more attention to economic stability than military advancement made Oyo vulnerable to invasion by the Fulani and at the same time unable to hold on to its tributary states.

To the west was the Dahomey kingdom which came into existence around 1625 and rose to prominence in the eighteenth and nineteenth centuries (in the region of present-day southern Republic of Benin, not to be confused with the Benin Empire). The kingdom was a form of absolute monarchy unique in Africa, contrary to more consensual governance in other Kingdoms, Dahomey was an absolute monarchy with a rigidly stratified society of royalty, commoners and slaves. It had a centralised bureaucracy into which commoners could move. At the courts, male officials had female counterparts monitor their activities and serve as independent advisors to the king. Conquered territories were integrated through marriage, laws and a common tradition of enmity towards the Yoruba to which it eventually ended up paying tribute.

With its wealth status and regional importance directly connected to the Atlantic slave trade, Dahomey was organised for war which was also crucial to its boundary expansion. Slaves captured from raids were either sold to the Europeans in exchange for weapons (rifles and gunpowder), cowrie shells, tobacco, pipes and alcohol; kept to work on royal plantations that supplied food for the army and court or used as human sacrifices during traditional festival celebrations. In the end, just as its rise coincided with the expansion of the slave trade, its decline coincided with Britain's pressure to end the overseas slave trade. This included imposing a naval blockade against Dahomey and enforcing anti-slavery patrols near its coast.

While Dahomey managed to transition from the slave trade to palm oil, with slaves kept to work on palm plantations instead of being sold, trading palm oil was far less lucrative than trading slaves. Around the same time, French control of Porto-Novo and Cotonou attracted coastal trade to those cities to the detriment of Dahomey. After the 1850s, Dahomey began experiencing territorial tensions with France resulting in two wars in which Dahomey was defeated and absorbed into French West Africa as the colony of French Dahomey with its capital at Porto-Novo.

The Akan states comprise a complex settlement of the Akan people in the historical gold-producing forest states in western Africa. The Akan people are several related ethnic groups located throughout much of what is now the nation of Ghana and parts of Togo and Ivory Coast. Their genesis is linked to the gold trade of the ancient Ghana Empire, north of present-day Ghana, which influenced the establishment of the earliest Akan states (such as Bono in the north, Asante in the south, and others) in what came to be known as the Gold Coast.

This Ashanti-European trade had begun at the turn of the eighteenth century and was instrumental to the military expansion of not only the Ashanti but also every dominant Akan state—selling slaves financed and armed the military, weakened the enemy from which the slaves were captured and provided the labour for gold mining and the agricultural production of yams, cassava, cocoyam, plantains, fish, game and some livestock. By 1820, the Ashanti Empire controlled a large area organised into three distinct regions. The Ashanti monarch, whose authority was symbolised by the golden stool, administered his vast empire through a general assembly, treasury and tax officers and executives.

Invasion by the British led to the decline of the Akan states, especially Ashanti. Despite claiming an initial victory over the British in 1824 and negotiating a 30-year peace period in 1831, they succumbed to the superiority of the British military in 1874. However, their final undoing was their refusal to become a British protectorate, which led to a British invasion in 1895 under the pretext of failure to pay the fines levied on the Ashanti monarch after the 1874 war. Following a British victory, the Ashanti were forced into a treaty and annexed into the British Empire in 1896.

Central African Kingdoms and Empires

Like West Africa, Central Africa, was a region of sub-Saharan Africa which experienced considerable trade interaction with Europe in the years before European colonisation. In many ways, it was of special relevance for the transition from initial contacts between well-established African political entities and European states to colonial control by the Europeans. The interaction largely echoed the format between Europeans and other regions of the world, with trade being linked to military dominance, in a sense understandable because of the absence of international rules at the time.

Quite a few major African political entities had developed in Central Africa in the days before the European 'voyages of discovery' of the late Middle Ages and Renaissance periods. The Portuguese were the first, going southwards through the Gulf of Guinea and establishing initial contacts. Among the most noteworthy of such states was the Kingdom of Kongo, or the Kongo Empire, (located in present-day Democratic Republic of Congo (DRC) as well as northern Angola). Also of considerable importance on the southern verge of the Central African region was the Luba Empire (located largely in southern-central, present-day DRC) and the Lunda Confederation (located in the southern part of today's DRC, across north-eastern Angola and north-west Zambia).

The Lunda Confederation in particular was an important political link between the western and eastern regions of Southern Africa. For many years the relations between it, the Luba and the Kongo Kingdoms dominated events in the region of what is now north-central Angola and its borderlands with the south-central DRC. Early Portuguese travellers were told that all they had to do was obtain permission to travel from the rulers of the Luba and Lunda in order to have safe passage from what is now Mozambique in the east to the Angolan coast in the west.

The Portuguese were the first to develop extensive interaction between Europe and Central Africa. Expanding contacts from their bases on the Atlantic coast, their main focus was the southern area of the region from the mouth of the Congo River. The Portuguese presence gradually entrenched and consolidated with the establishment of the Portuguese colony of Angola extending from the mouth of the Congo River southwards and eastwards into what is generally regarded as southern Africa. While what became present-day Angola was one of the earliest European colonies, the largest single area of Central Africa eventually came under

Belgian control at the end of the European 'scramble for Africa'. Initially the personal property of the Belgian king, it was later transferred to the state as the Belgian Congo (later DRC). The areas of Central Africa north of the Congo River became French colonies shortly before the Belgians established themselves in what is the centre of both the region and the continent.

The Central African region in many ways epitomises the historic range of events characterising the evolution of the Europe–Africa relationship. The Kingdom of Kongo has traditionally been a key political entity in the centre of Africa, straddling the mighty Congo River near its mouth on the Atlantic Ocean. At the time when the first recorded contact with Europeans took place, the Kingdom of Kongo was a highly developed state with a strong economy at the centre of an extensive trading network. The kingdom had already become a great producer of many natural resources and ivory as well as manufacturing and trading copperware, ferrous metal goods, raffia cloth, wooden products and pottery. In the early days of contact with Europe, there were many visits by diplomats from Kongo and other officials to Europe, starting in 1483. In 1485 the king of Kongo himself, Nzinga a Nkuwu, sent a large group to Portugal led by the nobles who had previously gone to Portugal. This group spent four years in Europe studying Christianity before returning along with Roman Catholic priests and Portuguese soldiers in 1491. Nzinga a Nkuwu was subsequently baptised along with his leading nobles and took the name João I in honour of the then Portuguese king João II. Christianity had subsequently a strong influence on the administration of the kingdom. By the end of the sixteenth century, the Kongo King Alvaro worked especially hard to Europeanise Kongo.

Tensions between Portugal and Kongo continued into the seventeenth century, especially given the stronger role of Portugal in Angola and in 1622 the first Kongo-Portuguese War began. In the wake of the Portuguese defeat, King Pedro II wrote to the Dutch States General proposing a joint military attack on Angola with a Kongo army and a Dutch fleet, funded by Kongo in gold, silver and ivory. Hostilities continued and by 1641 the Dutch captured Luanda. This was subsequently followed in 1648 by Portuguese reinforcements from Brazil forcing the Dutch to surrender Luanda and withdraw from Angola, allowing the new Portuguese governor to make peace with Kongo but demanding the Island of Luanda, the source of Kongo's money supply of nzimbu shells.

Throughout the eighteenth into the nineteenth century, the variety of interactions between Europe and Kongo increased, with relations between Kongo and Portugal once again turning hostile in the nineteenth century. In 1839, the Portuguese government abolished the slave trade south of the equator which had so damaged Central Africa, removing many of the negative factors which had for a long time damaged especially the Kongo-Angola region northwards into West Africa. For Kongo a commodity trade replaced the slave trade, initially focussed on ivory and wax, but this gradually grew to include peanuts and rubber.

At the Conference of Berlin in 1884–1885 when European powers divided up most of Central Africa. Portugal claimed and obtained a large share of what remained of independent Kongo in the wake of its previous occupation of much of the kingdom. It was nevertheless Belgium which eventually obtained the rest of the Kongo kingdom.

Located to the south of the Kongo Kingdom, the Ndonga Kingdom in present-day Angola was historically a prominent state with its own network of trading as well as political relationships with a variety of neighbouring peoples. Its geopolitical location led to Ndongo having well-established relations with Kongo, as well as the Luba Empire and Luba and Lunda Federation before the Portuguese arrived. However, it was with Portugal that Ndongo was destined to have the longest-lasting relationship, with it becoming a cornerstone of the Portuguese colony of Angola. The early development of the interaction between the Portuguese and both the Ndonga and Kongo Empires became a very important aspect of European involvement in Africa.

Southern African Kingdoms and Empires

Southern Africa has a history that is probably as old as time itself. Archaeological discoveries leave little doubt that the region was among those at the forefront of human development and technological innovation for millennia in prehistoric times. The history of community settlements indigenous to Southern Africa can be traced from the evolution of homo sapiens, through to the Stone and Iron Ages.

Many of the indigenous people were traditionally nomads. In many cases, more established social entities developed, including kingdoms which in some cases impacted vast areas. It should nevertheless still be borne in mind that the nomadic Khoi people in the southern parts of the region had cattle whose origins indicate an ancient bloodline related to the cattle of ancient Egypt, underlining the depth and extent of pan-African heritage. Some of the other indigenous peoples in the region had extremely sophisticated social systems with settled communities practising agriculture with or without extensive livestock. Some interacted with the broader, international, economic community, not only in the region but elsewhere with a special focus on the Indian Ocean, long before the advent of European colonialism led to a new, international structure of the region which displaced the old one.

The Portuguese led the way to an entrenched European presence in Southern Africa, including the establishment of the Portuguese colonies of Mozambique and Angola, but it was the Dutch who ultimately had the longest-lasting European influence on the region through the establishment of their support station at Cape Town. Although not intended as a colony of the same nature as the European colonies being established at the same time in the Americas and as the Portuguese envisaged in Angola, the Dutch presence led to the most extensive European involvement in Africa. Long-lasting legacies included at least two identifiable groups of South Africans, primarily of European origin, who although not indigenous Africans, developed in Africa with no other national affiliation. While there were times they could be regarded as part of a colonial narrative, this is offset by the African identity they have developed.

This is particularly pertinent to the one group descended from the Dutch Burgher society of the time of Dutch control, more specifically that of the Dutch East India Company, in the southern Cape. This group were soon generally known as the Boers and by the early twentieth century were known as the Afrikaners increasingly having a unique language and identity. These burghers, or so-called Boers, gradually established their own society although some chose to retain their strong connections with Europe and the Netherlands in particular. As they moved into the interior during the nineteenth century, they often participated in wars with or against indigenous peoples on terms reminiscent of historical times when Europeans and Africans were perceived as equals and also often formed alliances to fight other indigenous groups.

However, the fact that the aforementioned White African group, the Afrikaners, not only identified with Africa as a primary location of origin but also over the years incorporated many local words, practices, etc. endorses the importance of socialisation in the creation of group identities. In the case of the Afrikaners, in the formative years, there were also quite a few formal marriages with indigenous Africans (and in Dutch times also with Asian slaves who were usually freed by their new spouses).

It must be noted here that there is a counterpart for this European diaspora in Africa. In the course of the growth of interaction between Europe and Africa, especially during the past three centuries, there has been an accompanying growth of groups of Afro -Europeans in many European countries. Before the advent of nineteenth–twentieth century racist theories and attitudes, it was not uncommon for Europeans to have African ancestry, some prominent ones, such as the first prince Alessandro di Medici in Italy or the Russian poet Pushkin. These (forgotten) Afro-Europeans were found in all walks of life, from domestic service to high positions at royal courts, and were the precursors to the African diaspora resulting from colonisation.

Of all the indigenous kingdoms that developed in Southern Africa, one of the most noteworthy is that of the Zulu which was largely created in 1816 by Shaka kaSenzagakhona, a military commander of the then much smaller Zulu kingdom, through the amalgamation of a confederation of many small Nguni clans under Zulu hegemony. The original Zulu Kingdom had been founded in the mid-sixteenth century and in 1816 was already a leading political entity in south-east Africa being a key component of the Mthethwa Confederacy, or Empire, which in the eighteenth century ruled the region of south-east Africa to the immediate south of what is now Maputo.

The Zulu had a well-developed culture but were especially known for their good military system, largely created by King Shaka. He established new regimental structures and weaponry as well as tactics, making his troops discard their previous (ancient Egyptian-style) sandals to fight bare-footed, building an integrated standing Zulu army with conscription. It was this military might, backed by a strong political structure, that was key to the Zulu subduing many other peoples in the region. In the process, they depopulated vast areas of central southern Africa with raids into the interior known as the Mfecane ('scattering' or 'crushing') as well as carrying out raids far to the north. Remnants of the nineteenth-century Zulu Empire established new tribes far afield in such regions as modern-day Mozambique and Malawi.

In the nineteenth century, the Zulu began to intensify contact with both the Dutch settlers/Boers who moved into the then depopulated interior of what is now modern-day South Africa and the British who began to occupy locations of the country of the Zulu in the mid/late

1800s, beginning at the coast. This eventually led to hostilities and the first Anglo-Zulu War broke out in 1879. The British were defeated at the Battle of Isandlwana but eventually, the British defeated the Zulu and prepared for the two wars which soon took place against the Boer republics in the Transvaal and Free State. The second of these wars led to especially extensive collateral suffering for many of the indigenous peoples although many fought alongside the Boers together with volunteers from many continental European countries while the British were supplemented by forces from the colonials in the Cape and the British Empire.

As regards more ancient civilisations in Southern Africa, Mapungubwe located on the northern border of present-day South Africa near the Limpopo River which marked its northern borders with Zimbabwe as well as Botswana, is of key importance. Mapungubwe's establishment, like others such as Great Zimbabwe, may be linked to peoples who settled in the region about a thousand years ago rather than being the product of evolutionary processes of those who had always inhabited the area. Newcomers would nevertheless undoubtedly have blended with earlier inhabitants.

Dating back to around 900 AD, Mapungubwe was an iron-age settlement and kingdom. Without any contemporary written records, the history of Mapungubwe, its socio-political structure, economy and trade, wealth and decline have been pieced together from archaeological finds. Its society, thought by archaeologists to be formed by Bantu-speaking pastoralists, is the first, strictly class-based, social system in southern Africa. That is to say, its leaders were institutionally far higher in rank than and separated from its inhabitants.

In southern Africa, all kingdoms relied on a similar model of crop and animal agriculture which created plenty of food and surplus used in trade for needed goods with other regions accessed through the Limpopo River. Also, the discovery of glass beads, almost certainly from India and fragments of Chinese celadon vessels as well as gold in the burial grounds of Mapungubwe elites indicate trade with other states on the coast that passed from south-west Zimbabwe to the coastal city of Kosala. Indeed, Great Zimbabwe may have initially been a client state of Mapungubwe.

In the end, the kingdom is thought to have declined from a combination of climate change, overpopulation and shifting trade routes. Towards the end, changing weather conditions resulted in a series of droughts, whilst overpopulation put too much strain on local resources and the land could no longer sustain traditional farming methods. The inhabitants were obliged to disperse to the Kingdom of Zimbabwe which had begun to prosper in the north and would succeed Mapungubwe as the dominant power in the region.

Great Zimbabwe's expansive trade routes spanned the East African coast to India, with important ports at Mogadishu in present-day Somalia and Kilwa, south of Zanzibar. The proliferation of Asian and Arab goods, the practice of economic domestication and the mining of minerals—gold, copper and iron—were a dominant part of the Zimbabwean economy. The kingdom's capital was Great Zimbabwe, which was constructed in the eleventh century and continued to expand until the fifteenth century is located near what is today the town of Masvingo. Great Zimbabwe's most impressive edifice, commonly referred to as the 'Great Enclosure' is the largest heritage structure south of the Sahara Desert. By the 1400 s AD, a combination of factors was thought to have been responsible for the kingdom's decline marked by a mass migration of people. Lack of food and resources and depleted gold mines are some of the popular reasons historians have cited. To stave off this decline, Zimbabwe is thought to have tried to take over new regions with fertile soil and gold mines and also tried to secure better trade routes.

By 1550 AD, the whole of Zimbabwe was absorbed into the Mutapa kingdom, with only a few outlying settlements inhabiting the ruins of Great Zimbabwe. The new kingdom became a great empire encompassing most of its lands till the Indian Ocean. The kingdom expanded on the industry and trade that had made the preceding kingdom of Zimbabwe formidable. The Mutapa Empire continued to expand and by the time the Portuguese arrived on the coast of Mozambique in 1497 AD, believed to be in search of its gold mines, the Mutapa Kingdom was the premier state in the region, having reached its peak in 1480 AD, a mere 50 years after its creation. The extent of the kingdom's gold inspired European belief at the time that the region held the legendary mines of King Solomon. The Portuguese were able to establish permanent markets to expand their political influence which was only partly successful. The new trade routes established by the Portuguese along the Zambezi Valley from the coast of the Indian Ocean were built on previous use of the Zambezi by traders from earlier times.

A key settlement and trading centre on the Zambezi for the Mutapa Empire, also for its dealings with the Portuguese, was the village of Sena now located in modern Mozambique, linked to the Lemba nation of southern Africa. The Lemba claim historic interaction with the Middle East, including having forebears from that region who came southwards as traders, with specific strong ties to the ancient city of Senna in what is now Yemen, lying west of the capital Sana'a.

Control over the lower Zambezi Valley which the Mutapa Empire transferred to Portugal gradually made the area a key component of the new Portuguese colony of Mozambique. Mozambique was established with an extensive Indian Ocean littoral that bore witness to the key relevance of trade, while subsequently giving Mozambique an important geopolitical position straddling the transport routes between the Indian Ocean and much of the interior of Southern Africa. It was this interior of Southern Africa which, with the exception of the southern regions of what became the Belgian Congo, was controlled by the British by the early twentieth century thus joining up with South Africa at the extremity of Southern Africa.

While trade focussed more on Asia than Africa had been a key initial driving force for European settlement and colonisation in Southern Africa, as had happened in most other parts of the continent, the parallel growth of European interest in the economic benefits of dealing with Africa itself along with the overall geopolitical relevance of Africa was given considerable impetus by the economic relationship with Southern Africa. The discovery of diamonds and large deposits of gold at the end of the nineteenth century and the economic development of the region into the twentieth century were key factors underscoring such a growth in European interest. This played a major role in the reformatting of the economic relationships and situation for the region and Africa as a whole with the interests of European economies being the key focus.

East African Kingdoms and Empires

Most of the present-day north-east region of Africa was known to the Egyptians as the Kingdom of Punt—'the land of the gods' which was a major trading partner for ancient Egypt. While the exact location of the Kingdom of Punt has been the subject of historical debate, it has generally been taken as the region of the Horn of Africa.

The broader East African region consists of the Horn of Africa, which together with its hinterland, in many ways is closely linked to the region of the Red Sea and Egypt, and the rest of East Africa with its geopolitical links to Central and Southern Africa. Its proximity to the Red Sea and the

Indian Ocean gave the Horn of Africa especially facilitated access to the world outside Africa, with Asia and Europe not being too far or difficult to reach. Records of the East African kingdom of Macrobia's interaction with Europe date back to around 500 BC. By the first century AD, neighbouring kingdom of Barbaria on the north-east African coast (which like its neighbour was established around 1000 BC) was commercially trading with ships that sailed the Indian Ocean and Red Sea carrying cotton cloth, cloaks, tunics, grain, oil sugar, ghee, copper and tin in return for aromatic gums, tortoiseshell, ivory and slaves.

There was also the kingdom of D'mt (Da'amat) that emerged around 980 BC in the region of present-day Eritrea and northern Ethiopia. During the second millennium BC, cereal grains and the use of the plough were introduced into the region, possibly from the region of present-day Sudan and the inhabitants south of the region migrated to dominate the rich northern lands of Tigray. It was here that the kingdom of D'mt was established. The kingdom's dominance to the west, resulted in the acquisition and control of key trade resources such as ivory, tortoiseshell, rhinoceros' horn, gold, silver and slaves which were sold to the Arabians. D'mt's decline after 300 BC, was traceable to wars and diverted trade routes which subsequently led to the emergence of a number of smaller city-states in its place. It was then unified with the inland trading state of Aksum in the first century AD.

Aksum, also spelt Axum, had its base in Tigray. In the third century AD it had become the vibrant cultural and economic metropolis of the Aksumite Empire, a regional power largely based on trade and sustained by its naval strength. Considered one of the ancient world's four great powers of the third century AD (alongside Persia, Rome and China), by the Persian philosopher Mani, the kingdom of Aksum, from its base in Ethiopia, spanned the area covering present-day Eritrea and eastern Sudan. At its height, Aksum extended its influence from its capital Axum to the port of Adulis on the Red Sea in the Gulf of Zula. This also included the trade routes in the Sudan and farther inland, west—and eastwards to the spice coasts on the Gulf of Aden. The Aksumite Empire even spanned the Red Sea into the South Arabian kingdom of the Himyarites in present-day Yemen.

Adulis, a famous Aksumite port frequently welcomed merchants who traded textiles, glassware, tools, precious jewellery, copper, iron and steel for slaves, ivory, rhinoceros horn, tortoiseshell, gold, silver, frankincense and myrrh. Aksumite coins have been excavated in locations as far as ancient Greece and India. In the early part of the fourth century AD, Aksum adopted the Christianity of the eastern Mediterranean, most likely from the trade communities around Adulis, opting to adopt the Christianity of the Coptic Church (in Egypt) rather than the Christianity proposed by Rome and Constantinople. Aksum had cultivated military as well as trading ties with the Byzantine Empire, with its capital in Constantinople and it is understood Byzantium to have provided logistical support including more than sixty ships to transport the Aksumite army across the Red Sea in order for them to conquer Himyarite Yemen and liberate parts of south-western Arabia from a Himyarite occupation.

In 543 AD, Aksum's international trade was weakened as a result of internal strife which allowed Persia to assume supremacy as well as the rise of Islam, which cut off Aksum's trade with the Mediterranean world. This in turn forced Constantinople into an overland trade route with India and Africa. All of its key commercial centres and revenue were depleted as a result of this as Aksum could no longer maintain its military infrastructure and its complex systems of administration.

In the years that followed, the kingdom of Aksum continued to decline and what was left of it was destroyed in around 960 AD and later taken over by the Solomonic dynasty—a line of Ethiopian emperors who, according to Ethiopian tradition, were descended from Menilek I, the son of the Israelite King Solomon and the Queen of Sheba, Makeda. The previous dynasty seems to have ruled over a mostly peaceful state with a flourishing urban culture, in contrast to the more warlike Solomonids that followed. However, it is known to have built some monolithic rock-hewn churches in the thirteenth century, for the most part it was unknown to the rest of the world and isolated from other Christian nations. In order to build an alliance against muslims states that threatened the Kingdom's existence, they opened talks with Rome, France, Spain and Portugal but nothing came of it. However, it brought Europe's attention back to the region.

In the centuries that followed, Islam spread to the peripheries of Ethiopian rule. So, the Ethiopian Empire waged war in all directions. Strategic garrisons were established to consolidate newly conquered regions and exports, especially of gold, ivory and slaves that were trans-shipped from Ifat to Arabia were heavily taxed. To maintain economic control over these regions, the Ethiopians created a system of gults, in which the specific holders of a *gult* were paid tribute by the *gult*'s inhabitants, though these measures were met with resistance.

As heads of the church, the Solomonic monarchs built and beautified churches and promoted doctrinal works. However, in the long term, the Ethiopian Empire's imperialism only ensured that the Muslim states rallied against it and became a formidable opposition at the same time as internal rivalries weakened the empire's ability to respond. The involvement of Ottoman Egypt and Portuguese traders further disrupted emerging events. Moving the empire's capital to the more centrally placed and secure Gondar in 1636 AD reflected the new geopolitical reality.

The late 1800s saw some Ethiopian high points at a time when events in the region had an increasingly international dimension. Emperor Menilik II (1889–1913) played an important part in all of these events, especially given his new drive to consolidate territory in his empire, unifying and expanding his control. In 1896 there was the defeat of an Italian invasion which was one of many times when the empire came close to being colonised by a European power. Ethiopia actually managed to remain the only African country, along with Liberia, partly a creation by the United States for returning slave descendants, not to be formally colonised by a European power.

The economy of the entire region of the Horn of Africa, especially along the Red Sea, had been stimulated and further internationalised with the opening of the Suez Canal in 1859, the Italian occupation of Eritrea and part of Somalia and the establishment of a British base in Aden along with a French supply base on the Afar coast. These events naturally were themselves part of the broader internationalisation of the region with the expanding interests of the Ottoman Empire in semi-autonomous Ottoman Egypt being especially important. Also of special relevance were the broader strategies of both Britain and France to improve their positions in the region which were being threatened by the Italians in particular.

The long line of Solomonid rulers tried to solidify a strong strategic position for Ethiopia and keep foreign interests on hold, which eventually ended with perhaps their most famous of emperors, Haile Selassie I (reigned 1930–1974 AD). It was during the reign of Haile Selassie I that Italy yet again tried to colonise his empire and in 1935 he had to flee the Italian occupation of what was then often called Abyssinia. Italy then combined Abyssinia with its recent colonies in Somaliland and Eritrea into what it called Italian East Africa. In the subsequent events of World War II the British army defeated the Italian occupying forces and Abyssinia's full sovereignty was restored in 1944 along with Emperor Haile Selassie. It was after 1944 that the country became formally known only as Ethiopia, itself an ancient name for the broader region including Abyssinia.

While the sub-region of the Horn of Africa has a particularly long and complex history of kingdoms and international contacts, the rest of East Africa has also had its share of both. As with the Horn, trading played a major role in the international contacts and here, too, the Indian Ocean facilitated such activities. Along the East African coast from what can be taken as the sub-region of the Horn, there were early settlements of the Bantu that built their farming communities on the coast. These communities became more sophisticated and eventually started trading with ships from Greece, Rome, Assyria, Sumeria, Phoenicia, Arabia, Persia and Egypt.

This in turn led to Arab settlements along the same coast and the subsequent growth of an Arab-African ethnic and cultural Swahili people who became a key component in a trade network that helped give rise to the so-called Swahili coast, a region that covered much of the coastal regions of present-day countries of Kenya, Tanzania, Mozambique and Comoros and city-states like Kilwa and Zanzibar.

The Swahili coast largely exported raw products like timber, ivory, animal skins, spices and gold. Finished products such as silk, porcelain, spices, cotton and black pepper were imported from as far as the East Asian regions of China, India and Sri Lanka. The Swahili coast also imported ammunition: arms, gunpowder, swords and daggers; silver and bronze; glass and stone beads, fragrances, cosmetics, paper and books and also religious specialists and craftsmen, among others.

The arrival of the Portuguese on the East African coast in the late fifteenth century brought a long era of foreign rule and disrupted previous economic relationships similar to elsewhere in Africa with the advent of European colonisation. In the case of East Africa, however, the Portuguese were expelled in 1698 by the Imam of Oman and Oman gradually expanded its influence and in some cases its direct control along the coast. Zanzibar became the main Omani settlement on the coast and at one time was the location of the palace of the Sultan of Oman from which he controlled the Omani Empire. The Omani influences on Swahili culture proved to be especially significant. The Omani presence later disappeared as happened with all forms of independent indigenous identity once a subsequent German and British colonial presence in this part of East Africa was established. As a result of World War I, the Germans gave way to a British colonial presence throughout this part of East Africa which is largely centred around Lake Victoria.

This entire area is closely linked geopolitically to the adjoining regions of both Central and Southern Africa. It also had developed kingdoms in pre-colonial times with these being particularly noteworthy in present-day Uganda, Rwanda and Burundi. In much of Kenya and Tanzania, traditional societies were, as in much of Southern Africa, generally less structured and often more nomadic.

In pre-colonial Uganda, the states which were particularly well-developed included those of the Buganda, Bunyoro, Toro, Busoga and Ankole Kingdoms while the Kingdom of Rwanda gained prominence by the eighteenth century. The earliest inhabitants were absorbed by the Bantu people.

By the nineteenth century, Uganda was frequented by many Arab traders and slave- dealers from the coast where Zanzibar had become a major hub for a Middle Eastern presence on the East African coast. The inhabitants of Uganda soon found themselves having to diplomatically handle both increased pressures from the Arab traders and Zanzibar for closer relations while contact with Europeans slowly began to become more frequent. The British presence especially was more evident, given the British nervousness of being outmanoeuvred by Germany in Uganda which was seen as the source of the Nile with a geopolitical location that could threaten Egypt and with it the Suez Canal and the British sea routes to India.

The role of the Ottoman Empire should be noted as historically it played a very important role in East Africa. This was especially the case along the Nile Valley into the region of the Great Lakes, more than the Horn of Africa. Its impact on East Africa was largely through its vassal state of post-1517 Egypt, along the Nile Valley into the East African region of the Great Lakes. The Ottoman Egyptian annexation of the territories of what are currently the state of South Sudan, and the northern part of modern Uganda became an important element in the affairs of the region. As such, the Ottoman role can be regarded as one emanating from both Europe/Levant and Africa itself. Its role was considerable across a broad spectrum of issues into modern times.

Conclusion

This survey makes clear that Africa has had a long and complex history predating the European colonial era when the Africa–Europe interface was very productive with trade and other economic relations being of special relevance. The role of leading African kingdoms and empires was as important in Africa as their counterparts had been in Europe in the past, illustrating that in these flourishing times, there was mutual respect mostly lacking during the colonial period, bar individual exceptions.

When the Roman Empire began to decline both in Rome and Constantinople, especially following the rise of Islam, many of the empires in Africa were thriving. It was a period of prosperity for the great empires of Mali and Songhai, for instance, which had access to the trans-Saharan routes and had adopted Islam. But Rome's impact wasn't finished quite yet. With the fall of Constantinople to the Islamic Seljuk Turks in 1453, Europe's last gateway to Asia, Europe was forced to seek alternative routes to Asia. This led to European 'Voyages of Discovery' including Christopher Columbus' exploratory voyage in 1492 and prompted the Portuguese to circumnavigate Africa.

These events had serious implications for the Africa–Europe interface and the trans-Saharan routes too. The resulting disuse of the trans-Saharan routes was a significant determinant of the collapse of kingdoms like Songhai whose prosperity was tied to the Saharan trade. The chaos that followed was, like in Western Europe following the decline and fall of Rome, the inevitable result of any society whose prosperity does not have sufficient diverse sources. The regions that benefited from the trans-Saharan trade routes declined and suffered a lack of competitiveness, inflation and productivity decline in key sectors, such as textiles, a crumbling way of life. However, Europe's discovery of new trading avenues meant that this period of African decline was a period of European expansion.

As Europe expanded and trade ventures with Asia increased, the Europeans needed ports along the trade route to restock and repair ships and trade. This led to the establishment of 'colonies', originally only trading posts, and in time, the colonisation of Africa, whose decline had made it ripe for it, though there was a lot of courageous resistance against the invaders who responded with brutality and destruction.

Across Africa, like the rest of the world, territorial expansion was synonymous with increased control over trade routes and resources. Territorial expansion was gained through violent conflict, seldom through family alliances, as sometimes in medieval Europe. However, some of the major problems with violent conflict, besides the collateral damage to infrastructure and the loss of human resources that are crucial to economic growth, are the infighting and lack of trust it breeds among warring kingdoms. The declining trans-Saharan trade only exacerbated the need for violent conflict as kingdoms fought to control the scarce resources remaining available. This lack of trust and need to conquer neighbouring kingdoms was exploited by Europeans as they pitted kingdoms against each other causing them to deteriorate further and lose their capability to withstand colonisation. Another factor was the weaponry needed to gain superiority in violent conflicts.

And this is where Africa was lacking in the struggle against European expansion. With far more advanced weapons, despite African military sophistication, strategy and bravery, Africans were completely overwhelmed by the superiority of weapons that the Europeans had gained inter alia from their trade with the Orient.

Often overlooked as an important reason for the success of European invasions, are health conditions. As the different European and African civilisations increasingly mixed, they not only exchanged items of trade, but diseases too. While the Europeans were unable to contend with malaria and sleeping sickness, they involuntarily introduced viruses and bacteria like smallpox, measles, typhus, syphilis, plague and cholera which Africans had no immunity to and that wiped out a substantial part of their population. Of particular note is the accidental introduction of rinderpest when the Italians brought European cattle into Ethiopia, which decimated African livestock.

However, it isn't possible that any one of these factors, or even the combination of some of them, was the reason for Africa's decline to the point where it was too weak to resist European colonisation. After all, none of these factors were unique to the continent. European expansion, for the most part, was driven by necessity rather than curiosity. So curiosity alone (something the Africans had, which, for instance, led to the disappearance of Muhammad ibn Qu of Mali at sea) may not have been enough to drive African intercontinental expansion. While these are questions that can only be raised in hindsight, the point is that the African continent was no different from any other continent. It had large empires, kingdoms and dynasties that existed for hundreds of thousands of years. It had diverse systems of government and constitutions like others. It had thriving economies, strong financial structures, currencies for exchange and even boasts of the world's richest man ever. Even the trading of slaves by Africans to Europeans, at its core, was not exceptional to the continent. Slavery is as old as human history and historically went hand in hand with conquest. Be it the Greeks, Romans, Persians, Egyptians, Malians, etc., when kingdoms conquered their neighbours, they very often made slaves of them and either put them to industrial, domestic, or military use or sold or gifted them to other kingdoms. This not only served to boost the industry or military of the conquering kingdom, but it also further weakened the defeated kingdom and reduced its chances of fighting back. To the Africans, there was nothing unique about the European demand for slaves, which many of the larger kingdoms had in surplus. European were themselves often enslaved too, the Moroccan rulers in particular had made a business out of, and so did the Arabs and Ottomans.

So, while every continent, like the societies, communities and kingdoms within it, is unique in its own way, the factors around Africa's decline are not unique to the continent, let alone the misconception that Africa was uncivilised; or according to German philosopher Georg Hegel (1770–1831), lacking both self-control and the capability for development and, thus, was no historical part of the world. On the contrary, Africans and Europeans have had their histories intertwined for centuries through partnerships, have existed for hundreds of millions of years and civilised societies that are almost as old as time itself. However, as events following the collapse of the Roman Empire have shown, Hegel's perspective of Africans represents a selective use of timelines that ignores the period when the situation of both continents was reversed. And so, just like with European states following Rome's decline, the kingdoms and empires in Africa had reached the stage of decline (decay) in what has been referred to as the life cycle of civilisations. And all the other factors simply contributed towards the completion of this life cycle.

While there are different explanations of why and how civilisations rise and fall, American historian and theorist, Carroll Quigley, in his book 'Evolution of Civilizations' described the birth and life of civilisations as a seven-stage system: mixture, gestation, expansion, age of conflict, universal empire, decay and invasion. His argument was that the rise and fall of civilisations, although not common, was a normal course and that civilisations begin to decline when whatever way they use to gather, distribute and grow their resources turns into a political process that aims to maintain itself regardless of its resource-gathering ability. It just so happened that the decline of African states coincided with the expansion of European states. And while the European interaction with Africans began as a partnership of equals, it quickly deteriorated alongside the decline and expansion of Africa and Europe respectively. Nevertheless, the fact remains that African states, though boasting vast territorial boundaries, economic viability and prosperity and advanced administrative and military systems, were sufficiently weakened to be taken over by European military invaders.

CHAPTER 3

Pillars of Africa's Ancient Economies

INTRODUCTION

Despite Africa's vast size and natural extremes, neither the Atlantic Ocean nor the Sahara has ever formed barriers isolating Africans from the world. Instead, they have served as bridges for goods, services, currencies and ideas between Africa and the rest of the world. Africa's trading with the outside world is a direct reflection of the extent of trading activities and alliances that already existed between African regions. The partition of Africa by European countries and the imposition of their nation-state model distorted these till today. So was Africa's entrepreneurialism and intellectual openness; a holistic world view facilitated the integration of new ideas into their own. For millennia, foreign traders had sought access to bountiful natural resources and merchandise available on African coasts.

Control over these highly sought resources led not only to the policies of wealthy African states (with GDPs arguably comparable to that of contemporary Europe, the Middle East and Asia) but it also gave African rulers leverage over trans-Atlantic and trans-Saharan traders, who had to respect the region's trading practices and conditions. It furthermore provided a platform for African rulers to negotiate and establish trade alliances and partnerships with international traders that benefited them financially, politically and territorially. So when European armies invaded

© The Author(s), under exclusive license to Springer Nature Switzerland AG 2023
A. Adewale and S. Schepers, *Reimaging Africa*,
https://doi.org/10.1007/978-3-031-40360-6_3

and occupied African countries with whom they had concluded treaties and alliances they violated international law.

However, the profitability of these relationships would eventually lead to an overdependence on international trade and trading partners to the detriment of local industry and institutions, thereby ceding the economic advantage and kickstarting the decline of African economies. African trading activities were predominantly those resulting from agriculture, manufacturing and mining. They used their various currencies to facilitate trade and the patterns of inter-African and international trade relationships that existed at the time.

Economic Structures in Pre-Colonial Africa

The changing balance of trade, income and employment in pre-colonial Africa were on the one hand greatly influenced by political, social and cultural institutions and on the other by the prevailing global demand and accruing commercial power specific to each era. These institutions were well developed and thriving long before any new European influence following the fall of Constantinople which stimulated the search for new trade routes to Asia. They determined not just internal economic activities such as manufacturing and agriculture, but also trade and trade relationships across the continent and with global partners. Some African kingdoms and empires had already established important trading relations with Arab and Asian states before any European involvement.

The ability to establish these global links was a reflection of the complex and thriving economies of the African regions. In fact, the market economies, though unique to certain regions, were comparable to those of European counterparts in the same historic times in terms of the accessibility, mobility and flexibility they offered. They were characterised by highly monetised and market-oriented agrarian and industrialised production systems but also by the inter-African and global trading alliances and multiple use of currencies according to the prevailing demand.

Although there were similarities between the political and social influences on economic structures and activities across various African cultures, the unique nature of each culture (albeit nearly impossible to capture individually) meant that trading activities and relationships were specific to each empire or kingdom.

While parts of Africa operated democratic-like systems of government run by a council of elders and other kinship and age-based institutions, great pre-colonial historic kingdoms and empires such as those of Mali, Songhai, Kongo, Ghana, Benin, Oyo, Ethiopia, Zimbabwe, Zanzibar, Zulu were centralised states under the rule of monarchs with hierarchical structures and a social elite, not unlike those in Europe in the same period.

This centralisation of leadership influenced social interaction, entrepreneurial economic activity and trade. Access to land for agricultural activities, for example, was based on land allocations by community leaders, since all the land belonged to the community, similar to European countries in the middle ages, before the advent of capitalist market economies based on private property.

Also, the political power and authority over trade, settlement and decision-making remained in the hands of these rulers and aristocrats who governed through complex administrative structures. For instance, after Mali was conquered in the fifteenth century and the subsequent expansion of the Songhai Empire, King Sonni Ali developed new administrative frameworks, installing war chiefs over each province conquered. He ran a central administration from Gao (the capital city) with an imperial administration and royal military council, overseeing the kingdom and war chiefs. Songhai rulers would even go on to develop a complex system of titles like Paymaster General, Overseer of the Royal Estates, Harbourmaster for the River Ports and Chief of Market who oversaw economic and trade matters.

What these rulers also had in common was the desire to globalise their kingdoms. Using ambassadors and envoys, rulers sought alliances for military expansion, defence and trade. In the process, they not only had access to weapons and exchanged goods but also techniques and skills in agriculture and manufacturing far beyond the continent. Kongolese diplomatic efforts in the 1640s exemplify this. Their ambassadors made frequent visits to Brazil, and envoys were sent to the Vatican, Lisbon and Amsterdam. While this was to help shore up their military power against the Portuguese and their Imbangala allies (a militarised society that appeared in the seventeenth century around modern-day Angola), it was also vital for trade, producing and distributing food and sharing ideas.

In this way, European and Asian powers, together with other African kingdoms, were seen as equals in the 'great game' and thus potential global partners for military and trade alliances.

Internally, these kingdoms were stratified according to nobility, wealth or professional status. This determined what kind of access they were given to resources, trade or protection. For example, nobilities and elites had priority access to provisions and were prohibited from being sold as slaves.

The *Nyantios* (a fierce warrior aristocracy) had access to the best water and benefited from the labour of poorer classes, not unlike Europe's feudal systems at the time. The elites were better positioned to purchase guns and knives for their protection and to enforce their power. The gold and jewellery worn by the upper class in the Gold Coast protected them from being captured and sold as slaves and some kingdoms (Benin and Akan, for example) outrightly prohibited the sale of citizens as slaves— only outsiders (such as prisoners of war) could be sold. And this decision was not without its repercussions as highlighted later.

Additionally, as indicated by the Songhai rulers, nobilities and elites were given strategic positions that influenced trading in these kingdoms. In the Gold Coast, the king's relatives oversaw the collection of taxes and duties at ports. In this way, the rulers controlled foreign access to trade and provisions such as water, livestock and grain, both in ports and on local markets.

Through these structures, rulers enforced their authority and European traders knew perfectly well that they could not live, work or trade without the affordance granted by the African rulers. By charging tolls and mediating long-distance trade, elites developed into powerful aristocracies and African kingdoms developed into strong centres of political and economic power.

Economic Activities in Pre-Colonial Africa

The key economic activities in pre-colonial Africa were trade, agriculture, manufacturing (or industry), mining and the human resources that make them all possible. And this remains the case even today.

Crops, Livestock and Fish

In pre-colonial Africa, the abundance of land compared to the population density allowed pastoralists to rove in search of grazing land without any conflicts with settled farming communities and farming communities could use extensive agricultural methods on the wealth of land available.

Innovation and adaptation made it possible to engage in commercial agriculture, despite the challenges of a hostile environment caused by environmental conditions unfavourable to production including pests and diseases that attacked crops and livestock and a scarcity of labour which was strictly regulated by royalty, status, family, kinship, etc. At the time, commercial agriculture meant family farms that did not employ paid labour but produced enough to be self-sufficient (subsistence production) and permit bartering.

The Fula people of Fuuta Tooro (a semi-desert region along the border of modern-day Senegal and Mauritania) who were traditionally cattle herders, for example, rose to power in the sixteenth and seventeenth centuries, in part bolstered by the increasing demand for hides by Atlantic traders, particularly the Dutch who often traded them in Italy where the leather industry was booming. Another example is rice-growing communities across what are the modern-day countries of Senegal and Guinea-Bissau that produced a substantial surplus, which was bought by slave-trading ships, thus challenging the notion of Africa's inability to feed itself during much of pre-colonial times.

As indicated earlier, Africa also gained access to skills and techniques in agriculture through globalisation. The introduction and spread of maize in Africa illustrates this. Referred to as the second agricultural revolution in Africa (the first concerned the cultivation of wild plants on a systemic basis), historical sources suggest that maize was introduced by missionaries and traders from Brazil in the sixteenth century. While its spread was slow, its yield per hectare was far higher than other cereal crops such as indigenous millet and sorghum that were prevalent at the time.

However, as maize appeared to be more vulnerable to unsuitable environments and bad weather, it affected different ecological regions in different ways. Thus, farmers had to be innovative about how they introduced and grew the crop. Whilst in West Africa it was integrated as a major crop, leading farmers to create complex fallow systems, in what is now called the Ethiopian highlands it was treated as a garden crop since it was considered too risky to invest in on a large scale.

Like maize, cassava originated from tropical America, and it was introduced to Africa in the region of what is now referred to as the broader Kongo River basin (and particularly the parts of the basin now in modern-day Angola) by the Portuguese in the sixteenth century. The Portuguese had started using cassava on military campaigns as a means of feeding troops after borrowing the practice from the indigenous people of Brazil.

Cassava flour was fed to their army during the slaving wars waged alongside their African Imbangala allies and soon enough, cassava was being cultivated on plantations in Luanda and it would eventually become an African staple. However, the adoption of cassava by the peoples of modern-day Angola, rather than simply for sustenance and commercial agriculture reasons, was of strategic military importance, since it was used by the armies to undermine the power of the contiguous Kingdom of Kongo which was the undisputed political power of the time.

The cultivation of both maize and cassava are examples of the ingenuity shown by pre-colonial Africans in adopting and using borrowed techniques and skills. It also highlights how agriculture was useful for displaying the strength of African kingdoms and rulers, and trading and collaboration with foreign nations.

Livestock was always another important part of African agriculture, and until today it is often seen as a sign of wealth and status. The vast open spaces allowed farmers and herders to benefit from nature's resources, while in some parts they had to move with the seasons. It remains up to the present times the key source of food for millions of people, though it was (and is) sometimes threatened by weather conditions, such as failing rainfall.

The accidental arrival of rinderpest, through the import of cattle by Italian colonisers in what is modern-day Eritrea and Ethiopia, had a devastating economic and social impact in the late nineteenth century. It spread rapidly throughout the Sahel, where the grazing lands were abandoned and people migrated, leaving it to become semi-arid. It went further afield, wiping out cattle, and wildlife, and even reached the herds of Southern African peoples. It was the cause of malnutrition and starvation for millions in the rural areas. The plague also had an effect on Africans' mindsets and on resistance to European colonisation.

Fishing was of course limited to the coastal regions and to the great lakes and rivers. The Atlantic and Indian Ocean with their abundance of fishing opportunities were exploited since times before the last century BC, but consumption was not limited to the catch area, there is evidence of trade in dried fish towards inland kingdoms.

Manufacturing

Global traders were attracted to African ports for far more than just agricultural products such as food, raw materials and animals or, later, the slave trade. Many different peoples across the continent manufactured and traded large volumes of products including fine cloth, craftwork, household wares and weapons which were touted as more durable than those from Europe.

For instance, cloth produced in the ancient kingdoms of Western and Central Africa was so widely exported throughout Europe and South America that it was considered as currency and used in exchange for other goods and services. Not only was cloth produced in very high quantities (in the city of modern-day Luanda alone, more than 90,000 pieces of cloth were being traded annually in the 1610s), they were created with renowned diversity and skill, with Kongolese fabrics surviving from the seventeenth century. The richness of contemporary African textiles and design can be traced back to these days. The import of textiles from Asia, by Dutch and Portuguese traders first, was the beginning of the decline of this sector as an important part of GDP.

The same applied for craftwork. From the sculptures that inspired European cubist art to the lost art for the wax casting of bronze, the brilliance of pre-colonial African craft is apparent. The continent was rife with smiths, carpenters, cobblers, tailors, masons and weavers whose craft not only attracted foreign interest but also impacted urban development, such as the twelfth and thirteenth-century potshard pavements in Ilé-Ifè.

These craftspeople influenced everyday life and religious practices with objects ranging from household items for everyday use, like salt cellars, candlesticks, pots, jugs, clay glasses, etc., agricultural and domestic equipment, and jewellery and adornments to symbolise religious and political power, to objects of worship at religious shrines.

They also made Africa a cradle of art, and not just a cradle of mankind. African rock drawings, dating thousands of years ago, like European ones, seem to have some stylistic comparison; they give an insight in the thoughts of these people about the world they lived in. The crafts in Africa did not develop into a separate art category as in Europe. It was not until the nineteenth century that Europeans started to admire their design quality and to buy, exchange, or steal them. This ultimately led African crafts to become a principal source of twentieth century art in the West, which then changed the outlook on these objects. They had previously only a religious, political or social significance and this was sometimes discarded after their ceremonial use, while others were considered imbued with spirits, mostly of ancestors.

Their creativity was evident not only in the beauty, diversity, durability and quantity of their wares (as most of the production was done by hand, without machinery), but also in their technique. This is embodied by the magnificent ancient Benin bronzes already noted in the previous chapter. Apart from the famous plaques, portrait heads, and jewellery other smaller pieces (like depictions of the Portuguese alongside some of the trappings of their trade—books, jugs, cups, horses, etc.) were also produced using the lost wax technique.

Together with agricultural implements, domestic tools and other metal goods, local smiths also specialised in manufacturing weapons which included bows, arrows, harpoons, assegais, breastplates and swords. These were used to complement the weapons purchased from foreign trading ships both for warfare and individual protection. However, over time, weapons manufacturing became more sophisticated and advanced alongside military technologies to the production of steel arrows (from Timbuktu), muskets and gunpowder (from the Hausa kingdoms) as local kings sought to develop their political and military infrastructure.

Mining

At its core, the European scramble for Africa which particularly gathered momentum in the nineteenth century was to gain access to gold, later to other minerals. As early as the fifteenth century, gold was central to European expansion and its image of Africa as the 'golden country', with Mansa Musa, the Emperor of Mali (1312–1337), depicted as the custodian of the gold nugget. The golden country's popularity was a direct reflection of the abundance of gold, advancements in gold mining techniques and the boom in gold production, speculated to have been triggered by Mansa Musa's well-known pilgrimage to Mecca via Cairo.

Thus gold mining was not only a major occupation that was crucial to the economy, wealth and military expansions of regions on the African continent, but it was also one of the oldest and most important industries on the continent. For example, gold production in the pre-colonial region of Zimbabwe and the Kilwa states before 1500 is thought to have been around 1.5 million ounces a year.

Aside from gold, Africans also specialised in mining copper, iron, tin and salt, among others. Mining (the removal of minerals from their natural geological environment and their transport to the point of processing or use) and its associated metallurgy (the science of removing valuable metals from an ore and refining the extracted raw materials into a purer form) in Africa dates back around 12,000 years.

Mining was done through scavenging, alluvial/open mining and underground mining. Gold dust, for example, was melted in crucibles to be consolidated into ingots and reworked for a variety of purposes. Despite differences in mining techniques and when metallurgy was adopted across various African regions, the techniques of mining were very similar in terms of space and time and were constrained by similar factors such as lack of pump water. On the whole, mining activities, especially for gold, were jealously protected to safeguard the commercial advantage they helped secure.

While it has been argued that the lack of technological inventions and investments placed the continent at a disadvantage in agriculture and manufacturing, counterarguments purport that though Africans were aware of the technologies, they rejected them outright.

Although they accepted European imports like religion, agricultural produce, fabrics, skills and techniques, etc., based on the quality and quantity of their own end products, they believed they had no use for the technologies they rejected. The only European technology generally accepted across the continent was that relating to guns, reflecting the structural focus of African kingdoms on military, and consequently, economic expansion. Together with other imports they accepted, guns were integral to inter-African and global trade at the time, and in fact, a source of their undoing, because they never managed to acquire enough weaponry to resist the better-equipped European colonial armies.

Currencies in Pre-Colonial Africa

Contrary to general assumptions, economic historian Toby Green has convincingly shown that the first economic exchanges between Africa and the rest of the world were not through barter but were monetised. The stereotyped view of Africans bartering slaves for baubles rather than coins is completely wrong. At the time, currencies accepted included a variety of materials, including iron bars, cloth, cowries, copper and gold.

The use of these materials for trade was not particular to Africa or African relations but were a normal aspect of monetary exchanges during this period of history, accepted in Europe, South America and Asia. The possession of these currencies and the commodities meant that they could be exchanged (as raw materials or through production), as well as helping the growth of the global demand for the materials used as currencies, with this forming the crux of trans-Atlantic relations and determining the profitability of ports and viability of partnerships, including the growth and exchange value of the currencies.

Dating back to between AD 270 and 630, rulers of the then-great kingdom of Aksum in modern-day Ethiopia produced their own, round coinage to facilitate trade with the Roman and Byzantine Empires. Even regions without links to the Mediterranean world had already developed their own local currencies based on the natural resources and tools at their disposal. This was quite different from the barter system of payment in exchanges or kind for personal consumption. Rather, it was driven by the expectation that recipients would use the money for further exchanges, hence the requirement of general acceptability. A good example is cowrie shells. It is believed that they were already introduced to the continent as a general form of money as early as the eighth century by caravans of Arab traders. By the fourteenth to fifteenth century, they were being used across Africa as a form of money for local transactions, which led to their popularity to such an extent that European traders, in the seventeenth century, began to ship shells from India to supply the West African economy. Thus, before the advent of trans-Atlantic trade in the sixteenth century, Africans had already developed various forms of currency and exchange that coexisted together, some of which persisted up until the twentieth century. Some of these currencies are described below.

Considered one of the most successful and universal forms of money, cowry shells were a well-recognised medium of exchange and payment throughout Africa, Asia, Europe and Oceania. In West Africa, they were furthermore predominantly used as money. While Africans were accustomed to multiple currencies coexisting on the markets, cowries were preferred as they were easy to handle or move around and count. In addition, they were non-perishable, instantly recognisable and difficult to forge and suitable for all kinds of purchases, both big and small.

King Gezo of ancient Dahomey, located largely in the modern-day Republic of Benin, is recorded as having expressed his preference for cowries as currency because by using them he felt that he would always receive a fair price. The shells were used for everyday transactions to buy necessities like tools, medicine and cattle as well as for bulk inter-community and long-distance inter-African trade. In addition they were used to purchase slaves and provisions for trading ships for transatlantic trade. African rulers also used them to collect taxes, levies and fees.

Beyond economic and transactional value (which existed until the twentieth century), cowries also held social and religious connotations. They were a symbol of wealth and power and to this day they have retained their spiritual value as protective charms and amulets, mediums of divination and as payment for ritual services and ornamental value, being incorporated into jewellery, on cloths, worn in hair and decorating statues and baskets. And although cowries no longer serve as currency, traces of their history as a form of money remain in West Africa. For example, the Cedi of modern-day Ghana is named after the cowrie (in the Twi) language) and in modern-day Burkina Faso, people are still known to occasionally give alms to the poor in cowries mixed with coins. What's more, the West African Central Bank's headquarters in the modern-day Republic of Benin is decorated with cowries the size of windows.

As with cowrie shells, in many parts of pre-colonial Africa purchases, taxes, dues and fines were paid in cloth. These practices took place in such areas of Africa as those of the ancient Kingdom of Kongo now split between modern-day Angola and the Democratic Republic of Congo (DRC) and the ancient Kingdom of Loango in what is now the western part of the Republic of Congo (ROC), southern Gabon and the Cabinda region of modern-day Angola. Such practices also took place on a particularly extensive scale in the savannah regions of north-west and northern East Africa between the desert (where no cotton can be grown) and the so-called geographical 'Middle Belt' (where the use of textile clothing was less known until the twentieth century).

Cloth being used as money is reported as early as the fourteenth century in the Lake Chad area, alongside various other currencies. While it circulated freely on east-west inter-continental trading routes, in Africa cloth currency (especially cotton) had a significantly higher value in the north, towards the desert (away from historic manufacturing centres) and it tended to be the preferred choice for northward transactions (usually representing the cost of transport) in exchange for other forms of currency or goods in the opposite direction. For example, a merchant from the region of the modern-day country of Burkino Faso, going to Timbuktu now located in modern-day Mali, to buy salt with cloth produced in his home area, would also use cloth to pay his way on the outbound journey. But on the return journey, he would prefer to use salt whose value increased as he travelled south, even if he first had to sell it to obtain local cloth money.

This sort of exchange also played out in trans-Atlantic trade—the English bought cloth from Portuguese ships around what is now often called the Senegambia region comprising the modern-day countries of Senegal and Gambia, just to use as currency elsewhere, making a 100% profit on reselling. The value of cloth was quantified in terms of length. Each region had a recognised length of strip that served as the basic unit for transactions, usually the length of the ordinary woman's wrapper. The value, so far as it can be estimated in terms of European money, varied from about one penny to three pence in the money of the time, depending on the area. A whole cloth formed a larger unit, usually made up usually of eight or ten strips, according to local conventions. In the region of Senegambia the unit was a double-width cloth or a pair of single-width cloths.

In time, cloth and its production were experienced as monetary forms of power, violence and control (especially through its links to the slave trade), with Africans and Europeans alike keeping accounts in cloth monies. Its value was transferred from one economic system to another, even appearing in people's wills in the New World as valuable items bequeathed to heirs. The recognition of cloth currency was such that by the seventeenth century, it served as a standard unit of currency at trading ports, reflecting a significant rise in different types of cloth driven by local production and demand—Barkcloth (in modern-day Uganda), Barafulas (in the modern-day Cape Verde Islands), Libongos (in the region of the modern-day city of Luanda), Pigne (in modern-day Guinea Conakry), Cundis (in the ancient Kingdom of Kongo), and Gabaga (in the ancient Kingdom of Borno), to name but a few.

This growth of cloth as a currency also illustrated local demand. Apart from its use as currency, cloth was also purchased as a commodity for social and practical purposes and to display identity, wealth, status and prestige. Cloth was purchased for basic uses like sails, clothes and sacks. Even children in the ancient region of the Gold Coast were taught to trade for cloth. They either panned for gold on the beach and in streams, or caught and sold fish for gold, which they used to purchase linen cloth for their own needs. As was already mentioned nobilities and elites dressed to display their status in society and ethnic groups dressed to set themselves apart from other groups. And while cloth as money declined in the eighteenth century, to the present day it retains its value in other uses.

But it was African gold that was extremely important not only to the African, but also the European economy. It was gold from the great pre-colonial empires of West Africa, such as Ghana, Mali and Songhay, which provided the means for Europe to take off economically in the thirteenth and fourteenth centuries, being a major factor arousing Europeans' interest in Western Africa.

While cowry shells, cloth and other soft currencies (like copper and iron) were convenient for smaller, everyday transactions and some large ones, dealing with huge numbers of them (especially cowries due to their popularity) in very large transactions, was inconvenient and expensive. The value of gold made it an ideal replacement for not just executing larger transactions, but also importing large quantities of soft currencies.

The abundance of goldfields around the West African coast made gold easily accessible for export and this turned West Africa (especially the Gold Coast, named after the commodity) into a global business hub as European traders earnestly sought to gain access to the gold trade. This access was particularly important as for several centuries prior to the arrival of traders like Antonio Malfante in the fourteenth century, gold from the region played a key role in financing the expansion of Mediterranean economies. Similarly, the gold of Europe and the Muslim world came from this region as enabled by the growth in production which facilitate ready-cash economies. Thus, European involvement in West African trade (including the establishment of castle prisons in major trading centres) was in response to the processes in the gold trade that had already begun in West Africa rather than shaping the emergence of a globalised world or capitalising on the trade in enslaved persons.

Gold was also the boon of inter-African trade, leading to new trade routes, the consolidation of important new states, new governmental structures, further urbanisation and manufacturing growth in West Africa, e.g. Mossi in modern-day Burkina Faso and the centres of Kano as well as Borno in modern-day northern Nigeria. This is illustrated by trading activities between Borno and the Volta River Basin (an important transboundary basin in West Africa across the modern-day territories of the Benin Republic, Burkina Faso, Cote d'Ivoire, Ghana, Mali and Togo).

In ancient times traders from the then-Borno bought gold from the region of the Volta with locally produced cloth (thereby growing cloth manufacturing in Borno) which they dispatched north to ancient Tripoli. Traders were needed to carry the gold, expanding foreign-trader communities in West African city-states and consequently, the presence of Islam. Meanwhile, in ancient Borno itself, new governmental structures were required to manage this trade, resulting in the relocation of the capital centre from Kanem, further south to Ngazargamu. Furthermore, a new Sarauta system was established at this time in Kano. This was a complex traditional mode of administration that combined Islamic values with pagan variables in a common framework and system. This demonstrates the impact on religious and political systems, infrastructures and trade partnerships of what appeared to be a simple cloth for gold transaction.

Gold was convenient not just for larger transactions but also for small ones in the form of small, square pieces of gold known as kackra used for purchasing everyday goods in markets and paying taxes to access trading markets. Thus, the use of gold as the common unit of value led to the growth of tax base which in turn enabled the ability of local rulers to develop their political infrastructure and invest in imported weaponry. Although gold was a standard unit of value, many regions of Africa (including West Africa) did not have easy access to it and, thus preferred other forms of 'soft currencies', one of which was manillas. This was especially the case in regions with geographies that did not facilitate hierarchical states covering large terrains—regions like the creeks and swamps in modern day Guinea-Bissau and the Niger Delta. Also, the increasing price of gold led to the proliferation of other currencies like manillas.

Manillas were produced from melted down copper, bronze or brass imported from Europe to spend in local economies and also used as raw materials for ornaments, weapons and tools. They were widely used in West Africa from around the sixteenth century long into the nineteenth century, not just as currency but also as symbols of status and social power.

As a currency, manillas were exchanged for gold, slaves and basic provisions such as yam, wood and water. They were also used as gifts between nobilities to access trade markets across regions and also added to existing stocks that were then used to create art, in wars or melted down to provide raw materials for local industry and (like other forms of copper) manufactured into valuable items like the famous Benin bronzes. In some places, they were even used as membership payments for secret societies.

The fact that manillas were used both as a traditional concept of money such as exchanging them for goods, services and other currencies and less traditional ones, including for social and ritual purposes made them a more exchangeable currency and led to increased wealth by facilitating the growth of the market. This made for richer towns on the coasts and in the interiors, expanding trade, and increasing the region's capacity to grow through the extraction of a tax base.

While gold has traditionally been of major importance copper however is another ancient and well-known medium of exchange. Alongside manillas (which were not limited to just copper), copper-based currencies like copper bars, rings, wires, bells, basins and copper ingots were the preferred medium of exchange in many regions. In fact, in most of Africa, especially in many hinterland communities, copper and its alloys, bronze and brass, were more valuable than gold.

Like manillas and other 'soft currencies', they were useful for other aspects of society besides currency and exchange, as they possessed ornamental, status and amuletic/magical properties. Among other things they were used to encourage fertility, ward off danger, decorate swords and other weaponry to penetrate the magical defences of enemies and protect the wearer from offensive charms. Copper was also used in a variety of royal regalia: spears, staffs, swords of state, drums hung with brass bells, long trumpets, bracelets, stools, chairs, and in some cultures, crowns or headdresses. These all helped to increase the value placed on copper and consequently, its demand and supply through the Atlantic trade.

Iron bars were used for economic exchanges in the same way as cloth and cowries. In the seventeenth century, they were the dominant standard of value across the greater Senegambia region (like cowrie shells were in ancient Mali, Songhay, Kongo, the Kingdom of Hueda and Benin), and a very important medium of exchange in other parts of Africa. Records from the 1600s describe how iron bars were used as payment by the Portuguese for domestic help as well as taxes and tolls for trade access, inter-African trade and in exchange for slaves, provisions, goods and other currencies. And like other soft currencies, they also had other uses, especially the manufacture of weapons and agricultural tools.

As expected, the diverse use of iron bars increased demand, especially in West Africa, which in turn established its importance as a form of currency. Although there was a long history of local production, this demand was, for the most part, matched by the European demand for slaves, provisions, gold and other currencies. Without doubt, trans-Atlantic trade increased the volume of ore available, with iron bar imports constituting roughly half the value of all European imports. More iron bars meant increased trade and currency, facilitating market exchanges. Because European negotiations were in response to West African demand, the terms of trade were set by West African rulers and their smiths, thereby exercising their authority over trading activities at their ports.

While European traders have been credited with the importation of iron bars as currencies into the African economy, as with cloth, iron bars pre-date their use in the trans-Atlantic trade in the region. The European traders only imitated an existing framework of currencies. By the later part of the seventeenth century however the use of iron bars (and cloth) as currencies had started to wane, being eclipsed by other forms of money.

The aforementioned examples are some of the dominant currencies that (co-)existed and facilitated trading and exchange in pre-colonial Africa. Others are brass/bronze rings, iron blades, salt (which was also used as a form of currency in the Sahel region), silver, beads, kola nuts, dye, etc. In some cultures, some of these still serve as a form of currency and exchange, for example, the presentation of kola nuts as bride price payments.

There are a number of themes that emerge from this summary of dominant currencies in pre-colonial Africa. Firstly, economic activities of currency exchange (including taxation), etc. already existed in Africa before trans-Atlantic trading began in the region. European traders only observed the pre-existing systems of economic trade, importing currencies they had access to in exchange for the currencies, goods or services they wanted.

Secondly, local kings or rulers were in control of trading activities at, and trade markets around, their ports. They set the rules that trading ships had to adhere to and restricted access to trade markets as they saw fit. As already alluded to, Europeans knew very well that they could not have lived, worked and traded on these markets without acknowledging African power.

This extensive summary of pre-colonial African currencies and the emerging themes highlight the prominent position of the continent, especially in international trade relations and creates a context for understanding the process and extent of its eventual decline.

Going Global

Trade relationships have always been presumed to be based on equitable exchange, of goods and services not available in their own region or country or far more expensive there. However, the general perception of pre-colonial, global relationships between the West and Africa has placed

Africa at a disadvantage, positioning the continent as having underdeveloped institutions, cultures, or anything else of value with future advances only being able to take place under the direction of Europeans.

On the contrary, pre-colonial African regions had well-developed and prospering political, economic and social systems as was recognised in many documents written by travellers and traders at the time. While these systems varied from European systems (being as they were influenced by different social, cultural and religious beliefs), as mentioned above European traders had to adapt their style of trade to these systems to gain access to goods and services, they crossed the Atlantic to acquire.

Even before European trade began, globalisation had come to many parts of the continent. Ambassadors from the state which was transforming into what is now modern-day Ethiopia visited the Chinese courts in around 150 BC. The then Ethiopia's feudal society, incidentally, had many features similar to Europe. African trade connections expanded rapidly, especially after 700 AD. Modern-day Madagascar was linked to China through the trading town of Kilwa (located on an island off the coast of what is now southern Tanzania and founded by a Persian sultan in the eleventh century). Lamu, in Kenya, was an important trading settlement of the Omani empire.

Over time, the continent attracted global traders seeking to exchange cloths, hides, iron, slaves and gold, among others, for weapons, Indian textiles, dye, alcohol and other European products. In today's estimation of value, this may seem an unfair trade, however, at the time, before the inflation of African currencies (as discussed later), it was simply an exchange of goods that were difficult to access in the own region or country, which was at the heart of both inter-African and trans-Atlantic trade.

Long before trans-Atlantic trading began, trade was necessary between African regions since each had its own geographical location, different terrain, natural resources and specific skillsets.

For instance, the thick rain forests of the Kingdom of Kongo were very different from the dry forest, savannahs and semi-deserts of most of the great kingdoms of West Africa. While gold was much easier to mine (apart from goldfields, tiny grains of gold could be found, sparkling in riverbeds after rainfall), regions around the savannah lacked the natural resources to obtain salt, and, thus, it was necessary to trade for it with people from the desert of Northern Africa where it was easy to mine salt. This further facilitated the trans-Saharan gold trade. The ancient kingdom of Ndongo, in modern-day Angola, though dry for the most part, had very fertile valleys where many crops could be cultivated and good terrain on which to raise cattle and oxen, which, together with hides, were traded in exchange for salt and other necessities.

This kind of trade relations existed across Africa—In pre-colonial times Borno traders exchanged locally produced cloth for gold in the Volta River Basin. Likewise, people from what is now the Dakar region of modern Senegal travelled by horse to the then port of Rufisque to exchange locally woven cloths and received traders at what is now modern Dakar who brought a mixture of ivory, yellow wax, gum Arabic, couscous and chickens to sell. Camel caravans from North Africa carried bars of salt as well as cloth, tobacco and metal tools across the Sahara to ancient trading centres such as Akan and Djenné and Timbuktu on the Niger River in exchange for gold, ivory, slaves, hides, kola nuts, pepper and sugar, to mention but a few.

Goods and necessities were not the only commodities that changed hands. As with every trade relationship, skillsets, ideas and social cultures were also exchanged. Historians note that before contact with Europeans, similar woodcarving techniques were found from the Yoruba regions to as far south as Loango. Carvings dating from the seventeenth and eighteenth century which originated from the then Kuba kingdom in the modern-day DRC in Central Africa depict the playing of warri, a game widely found further north in West Africa, as well as East Africa. Sugarcane, long cultivated in the eastern Mediterranean and Arab worlds was being grown in the Kingdom of Kongo before the Portuguese arrived. Also noteworthy is that people in West Africa already appeared conversant with the use of shell currencies, as has been noted earlier in this chapter, before the European trade began. This was possibly a legacy from the region having traded in more ancient days with North Africa, a region that had again long traded with the Arab world, taken together a practice that may help explain the traditional spread and influence of cowrie shells in West Africa.

It also explains the access of the Arab world to West African gold and slaves (as summarised later), and likewise the spread of Islam to Western Africa. Northern economies that traded with the Arab world were short of gold, but controlled salt mines in the Sahara. Whereas West African kingdoms had plenty of gold but needed salt, leading to the establishment of the gold-salt trade previously noted, which in turn made gold available for trade by northerners to the Arabs. Likewise, Islam and Arabic spread to Western Africa through established trans-Saharan trade routes and this was mostly accepted because they helped to increase trade and commerce through the market opportunities and credit facilities they offered.

Finally, geographical access to resources led to the creation of alliances between communities and kingdoms. Alliances kept ethnic boundaries fluid and minimised competition and conflicts that impacted cultural and ecological landscapes. For instance, the cooperation of hinterland people, who produced the bulk, wealth-creating products demanded by the international market, was needed by businesspeople on the coast to successfully acquire wealth.

The coastal elite, aware of their weaker bargaining position, rather than fight for access to these products formed alliances to secure access to them. In turn, people in hinterlands formed networks of alliances with each other. For example, the Taita and Akamba in the territory of what became modern-day Kenya, formed blood brotherhoods with the Waata to receive hunting poisons and magic that could augment their success at hunting elephants while the Waata formed alliances with the Oromo to receive protection and access to hunting.

Trans-Atlantic trade relations, like inter-African trade, hinged on what each side could access and negotiate in terms of currencies, goods, services, religion, food, social vices and ideologies. For instance, the main attraction of the Kingdom of Kongo for the Dutch was the trade in cloths and ivory while the Portuguese in the Gold Coast wanted either to secure access to the gold trade or gain supplies of food that assisted in their overall trading activities. Negotiations ranged from simple parleys (to agree on price and weights) to regional alliances.

Alliances were formed based on access to what each side needed, be it slaves, gold, weapons or currencies (to trade with other regions or build surpluses). They were maintained by exchanging gifts (especially from European traders to African rulers), preferential access to trading markets (granted to European traders), allowances granted (for Europeans to build fortified bases, for example) and security (of European traders' lives and property). Portuguese actors in West Africa for instance were known to frequently gift European cloths to African rulers in ancient Assay, Akan and the Gold Coast, while they depended on these rulers for their security, and the King of the Kongo was known to possess European tapestries in his palace.

More importantly, West African rulers formed these alliances to extend their economic and political power and strengthen their military.

Economically, trans-Atlantic alliances attracted more regional trade, which meant more taxable transactions and fines, increased wealth for rulers and possibly more geopolitical control over smaller kingdoms in the region. However, control over other regions was usually gained through military strength and access to European weaponry and cavalry, as African rulers sought to extend their territories, accumulate tributes and enslave smaller societies.

For their part, trans-Atlantic traders armed African allies in an attempt to gain a mercantile advantage over European geopolitical counterparts, which would often lead to direct conflict between them. This was not peculiar to traders on the West African coast. In the 1670s trans-Saharan traders, worried that the Atlantic trade was out-competing them, led from the north by Nasir al-Din, fought back against the European traders on the coast and many were killed. All the players in pre-colonial African trade were there to protect and promote their commercial interests, and what existed was a give-and-take relationship between Africa and the rest of the world.

The pursuit of commercial interest also defined trans-Saharan trade. On the one hand, the Arabs needed the gold Africa offered. Illustrating the importance of African gold to Europe in the Middle Ages is the fact that two-thirds of all the gold circulating in the Mediterranean region at that time is estimated to have been imported across the Sahara by North African traders. This made the uninterrupted continuity of trade more important to North African rulers than their West African counterparts, something which meant that they were willing to abide by the local conditions imposed by West African rulers.

West African rulers, on the other hand, were interested in the market opportunities and credit facilities the trans-Saharan trade offered. However, states to the west and north of the savannah which controlled access to neither salt nor gold, built their position by maintaining control over the principal trade routes leading from the terminals on the edge of the desert to the goldfields and on the route of the caravansaries in between. In this way, they could monopolise the trade, prevent the Arabs from making direct contact with the actual producers of gold and act as middlemen.

Items traded made up a significant part of the goods traditionally purchased as symbols of material wealth. Examples include such items as the aforementioned currencies, weapons, and liquor (especially brandy). Spiritual values also had a major impact on trade relations in pre-colonial

Africa and in this regard two religions were of special significance, i.e Islam and Christianity. The African traditional religions and worship of various deities across the continent also continued to strongly influence culture, social life, political structures and economics and trade.

However, the 'foreign' religions, Islam and Christianity, were critical for the expansion of trade beyond Africa's boundaries, Islam across the Sahara and Christianity across the Atlantic and Far East. Conversion to Islam helped merge diasporas of traders into a shared identity. Through these cultural links, the trade links and political systems were consolidated. Geographic divides can be crossed if there is a common cultural understanding. On the other hand, converting to Christianity (or at least promising to convert, or pretending to be Christian) was important for negotiating and securing alliances with the trans-Atlantic traders. Also, the sentiments attached to the display of gold in Christian cathedrals in Europe contributed to its demand and trade on West African coasts.

As with other conventional trade practices discussed, owning and trading in enslaved people, which existed in different forms, was part of an existing framework closely related to African kinship structures and imitated by the Europeans, who at the time were familiar with the concept of bonded labour in medieval societies; it persisted up to the nineteenth century in some parts of Europe. Various types of slavery existed, such as chattel slavery (where slaves were owned as property, including their offspring), domestic slavery (where slaves would work primarily in the master's house, sometimes even considered part of the household, thereby retaining some freedoms), debt bondage slavery (where slaves were exchanged as collateral to secure the repayment of debt), military slavery (where slaves were acquired and trained to serve in slave soldier groups). This is different from the enslavement of people through conquests.

From the beginning, violence and warfare had been associated with the slave trade. Enslaved war captives were paid as tributes, sold as commodities or given as gifts. This pre-dated the arrival of European traders who initially focussed on copper mines, goldfields, cloths and ivory. However, in East Africa, the slaves trade dates back to 284 AD. It had been in existence in the seventh century as Islam spread across North Africa, before Europeans arrived on the continent and before the first West African slaves were sold across the Atlantic, which will be the final phase of historic slave trade. Unlike the Europeans, for whom it was a long time of secondary importance, the capture and trade of enslaved persons by Arab Muslims was part of their primary trade interests.

Arab Muslims in Eastern and Central Europe and the Ottoman Empire had initially taken white slaves to sell them in Arabia, which needed extra labour, but the growing military power of Europe put an end to Islamic expansion, leading to a shortage of slaves. Part of this trade was in fact kidnapping for ransom, since they knew that churches and wealthy private families would try to buy them back. Therefore, Arab Muslims began looking increasingly to black Africa for their supply and they were aided by existing social structures and traditions that facilitated the purchase of slaves for their purposes. The Arabs made forays into the inner parts of Africa and brought back caravans of slaves to Zanzibar in particular. Captured slaves were sold to the Middle East to work as field workers, teachers or harem guards, (the reason for their castration). This explains the absence of a population of African descent there, contrary to the Americas, where slave owners wanted to have men and women to grow their workforce. And although Islamic legal views protect people from enslavement, this applied only to Muslims, including African Muslims who were not allowed to be enslaved, often a reason for conversion. By the seventeenth century, as more merchants from Oman settled in Zanzibar and it had become an international trade hub, the Zanzibar markets alone were handling as many as 70,000 slaves per annum. This was further aided by local customs officers who collected slave trade duties, wealthy merchants who financed the slave caravans and petty merchants who purchased and resold slaves kidnapped by Africans or Arabs from the hinterland behind the coast.

The trans-Atlantic slave trade, on the other hand, began around the 1640s in response to the need for labour on the Portuguese sugar plantations in the New World. Eventually, all the major countries across Europe joined in, making enslaved persons the main export from West Africa. What initially began as a simple trade of war captives soon evolved into raids on weaker regions by stronger ones, kidnapping and bandit raids for the sole purpose of trading with European slave ships. This was further enabled by the provision of arms, military support and credit facilities to bolster the raids and kidnappings.

The demand for slaves was such that, as early as the mid-seventeenth century, English ships would return from the Niger Delta region laden with as many as 400 enslaved persons at a time. This trade in slaves, unsurprisingly, strengthened the trade in other commodities like weapons and food (to feed slaves during transport). It also led to more prison castles being built, further consolidating the powers of African rulers whom the Europeans had to rely on for protection and access to basic amenities like water.

Although trans-Atlantic European traders initially confined their presence in Africa to coastal regions, their slave-trading enterprise affected African communities everywhere. Often through treaties and other means (purchasing from raiders, kidnappers or local slave traders), Europeans gained access to the East African slave market. For example, in AD 1776, the King of Kilwa (on the coast of modern-day Tanzania) agreed to a treaty in which he promised the French 1,000 slaves annually. The demand for labour in New World plantations also fuelled the traffic of East African slaves to what became the French-controlled island of Reunion lying to the east of Madagascar and the modern day country of Seychelles. In the early nineteenth century the figure rose to about 15,000 to 17,000 slaves per year. During the same period, fifteen to eighteen Brazilian slave ships a year would arrive in what is now modern-day Mozambique. It has even been suggested that shipping enslaved East Africans to the Americas began a bit earlier than the West Atlantic slave trade itself. The trade was carried out by Africans and Arabs and later by Europeans themselves.

The demand for slaves, and the acceptance of their value as a commodity, meant that like other commodity currencies, they were eventually treated as units of account. Enslaved persons were used as currency on both the transatlantic and trans-Saharan trade routes. By the eighteenth century, for example, the Hausa states of northern Nigeria were often paid for their literacy skills with captives. Connection to long-distance trade in captives brought to African societies the financial equivalence of bodies and currency that was at play in the regions of both the Atlantic and Sahara. Political and military superiority over neighbouring regions determined the alliances formed around the exchange of slaves.

There was opposition though. The kings of pre-colonial Benin, for instance, refused to participate in the Atlantic slave trade thereby placing it at a disadvantage to its neighbours who were happy to allow slave trading at their ports. This led to Benin being side-lined as ships instead traded with Allada, nowadays located in the south of the modern state of the Republic of Benin, centres along the geographical Bight of Benin in the Gulf of Guinea, and the Igbo-speaking Ijaw people of the Niger Delta region of modern-day Nigeria, i.e. the Kalabari Igbos, thereby growing their stocks of currencies, weapons and manufactured goods. Notwithstanding, trading slaves was one of the major determinants of the eventual economic decline of African states, because it depleted the workforce for more long-term economically viable activities in manufacturing or agriculture.

Finally, it is important to highlight the roles of women in trade in pre-colonial Africa. Traders were usually women in many parts of Africa, in particular in West Africa. Women worked, raised their own funds and were considered some of the richest people in their regions. They were both big traders and market hawkers, interacting with Atlantic traders on a daily basis. They traded in cloth and textiles, fine thread, calabashes, ceramics, a large variety of iron-craft, woodwork and edibles such as roasted monkeys, catfish, rats, parrots, fowls, yams, manigette pepper in pods or ears, dried lizards, palm oil, large beans, as well as various sorts of fruit, vegetables and animals for consumption, including live dogs. Women were also involved in producing cloth, agricultural labour and fishing for currency shells.

This shows the impact women had on the economy, including going on to hold political power in places like pre-colonial Dahomey (modern-day Benin Republic). Such evidence, therefore, suggests the need to rethink traditional stereotypes regarding female power, particularly in societies in West and West-Central Africa. A well-known example is provided by the 'Mama Benz' in modern-day Togo in the 1950s and 1960s. They traded in the cloth of African design and an ancient Dutch wax technique and became wealthy enough to allow them to drive a Mercedes-Benz.

The Economic Decline of Pre-Colonial Africa

The rise of slavery was one of the significant markers of the economic decline of pre-colonial African states. A major consequence of this trade was the shortage of labour in Africa to replenish the labour needed for the development of European economies in the Americas. The slave trade has widespread negative consequences on the labour market of West African kingdoms which hindered its competitiveness and commerce. The loss of labour meant that the economic output of the young men who created surplus value went to the growing European empires, as for centuries the slave trade with the Arab world had affected Eastern Africa.

On top of this, societal life was distorted at the micro-level as the targets for slave trading were usually its most healthy and economically productive members. As a result, farmsteads, villages and towns were abandoned on a large scale for a new, more precarious way of life. Raids and kidnappings for slaves led to fear and insecurity that minimised legitimate exchange and ruined inter-African alliances. This made the procurement of slaves, livestock and food through violence and warfare inevitable, continuing the cycle of fear and insecurity. The resulting migration and relocation of many people to move to fortified towns and the mountains, led to subsistence insecurity and it made people vulnerable to disease, famine and starvation. This was sometimes so extreme that parents reportedly sold their children into slavery for food.

Apart from the depletion of capable human resources caused by the slave trade and the ensuing internal deterioration of social and economic conventions, there were other, interrelated causes that contributed to Africa's economic decline.

In economic terms, African states lost out in the accrual of surplus value. While they acquired exorbitant amounts of a wide range of currencies, the multiple religious and social uses of every single currency for traditional worship, to display wealth and nobility, decoration, manufacturing, fashion, etc. demonstrated a worldview that did not see numerical surplus as a privileged, economic value isolated from other forms of social and moral value. Thus, rather than increasing their store of capital value and transferrable wealth, the African states only increased their exchange mechanisms which eventually positioned them at an economic disadvantage in negotiations with Atlantic traders.

As the demand for slaves grew, alongside the decline of Africa's negotiation power, local industries were swamped with massive, cheap imports from Asia and Europe in exchange for slaves. This resulted in the mass circulation of commodities that could have been manufactured locally, but local manufacturers were unable to compete with the prices of these imports. Even worse, global interests appeared to have shifted from the wide range of commodities previously exchanged to fixating on the acquisition of slaves and the associated, increasing loss of labour in African states.

All of this led to a decline in manufacturing for export and its attendant economic power, meaning that local currencies could no longer hold their own exchange value on a global scale. In the end, the combination of importing commodities (like cloth, copper basins and pans) that could have been manufactured locally, and the declining value of currencies as capital was accumulated elsewhere, led to increasing capital disparities between Africa and the global economy.

Increased importation of currencies without a balanced importation of products for trade created inflationary pressure on local currencies, making them virtually worthless on the global market. The diminished value of these currencies meant that Atlantic traders could dump large quantities of them on African shores as they were valued at next to nothing compared to the 'hard' and more stable currencies accrued. The spiralling devaluation of currencies also had drastic implications for the cost of commodities on the local market. For example, the cost of an enslaved captive paid for in cowries in Benin rose by 15 per cent, while the number of cowries used to purchase a load of yams increased from 8,000 to 89,000.

Inflation not only created a wider economic imbalance between Africa and Europe, it also accentuated the wealth and social disparities between the elite and ordinary classes of people in local regions.

The trans-Atlantic demand for slaves went hand in hand with increasing violence in the West African region. As noted above, violence of some kind was needed to continuously replenish the supply of slaves: war, raid, kidnapping or bandit raids, which the Europeans were willing to sponsor either through the supply and exchange of weapons or through credit facilities. This violence to serve the slave trade had consequences besides the constant supply of slaves (which in itself was instrumental to Africa's economic decline). Firstly, it led to a growing resentment of rulers and elites among subjects, which prompted revolts and, as in the Kingdom of Kongo, these unrests led to destabilisation of the monarchy and opened up the region to further exploitation by global forces.

These revolts, aggravated by the economic imbalance brought about by inflation, contributed decisively to the implosion of the Kingdom of Kongo by the end of the seventeenth century. Additionally, local trade was hampered by concerns over security due to bandit raids and kidnapping. And finally, European traders also benefitted from the ransom of enslaved persons for gold exports, further increasing their accrual of the hard currency. The dependence on Europe for political advantage and external trade to supply money meant that African states were required to meet whatever demand prevailed on the global market at any given time. Thus, as global demand shifted from cloth and gold to slaves, African rulers were compelled to adapt to the inordinate demand for slaves, whatever the cost, in order to maintain their political advantage and money supply.

This shift was driven by the currencies already accrued, together with the discovery of gold in South America, the economic impracticality of the cloth trade due to dwindling global demand and the need for labour on farms and plantations in the West. Thus pre-colonial kingdoms like those of Benin and Kongo, which were initially side-lined due to their refusal to participate in the slave trade, were forced to reverse their position and by the 1730s began to participate in the slave trade. This dependence on Europe also allowed trans-Atlantic traders to deliberately exploit African brokers with unfair trading practices. This included deliberately replacing exchange commodities by those that tended to create disorder, such as gunpowder and alcohol, having the upper hand in negotiating alliances, and strengthening their influence by pitting regions and kingdoms against each other. Overall, this put Africa at a disadvantage and forced it to participate in trade relations that were not just detrimental, but further widened the economic gap between the continent and the outside world.

The decline of the African economy, while intricately linked to the trade in enslaved captives, was also the result of greater economic and political inequalities within the continent itself, and greater inequalities between the continent and other parts of the world which were caused by inflationary pressure and the loss of negotiating power.

While Europeans played a key role in destabilising Africa's economy, in the long run, the continent's inability to consolidate its currency surplus, its attachment to traditional technologies and the disparities between the personal interests of the rulers across its many regions placed it at a disadvantage that would eventually result in its economic decline.

CHAPTER 4

African Pre-Colonial Social and Political Structures

INTRODUCTION

Insights provided on the nature of African society, starting with the basic socio-systems, values and then moving to the political systems they contain, are useful to help illustrate the sophistication of the African identity. As with all societies, there are inherent differences as well as similarities to European societies where individualism has progressed much farther.

The concept of the African family is illustrated in Nelson Mandela's autobiography 'Long Walk to Freedom' where he states, 'My mother presided over three huts at Qunu, which … were always filled with the babies and children of my relations. In fact, I hardly recall any occasion as a child when I was alone. In African culture, the sons and daughters of one's aunts and uncles are considered brothers and sisters, not cousins'. The concept of family in several African communities is not limited to time and space. It often involves multigeneration, relatives living far and near, the living as well as those who have joined the ancestors. In Africa today, the communitarian spirit is still more affirmed than in Europe such that a person does not exist in isolation but as a part of a community, hence the notion of Ubuntu—'I am because we are'. As Desmond Tutu affirmed, 'Ubuntu is open and available to others, affirming of others, does not feel threatened that others are able and good, based on a proper self-assurance that comes from knowing that he or she belongs in a greater whole and is diminished when others are humiliated or diminished when others are tortured or oppressed'. This basic fact lies often at the root of precedence given to family and relations over the legal institutions which is the modern (imported) state.

This in turn is based on the main principle of the African-centred worldview is the interconnectedness of all things. In line with the writing of scientists such as Frobenius and Talcott Parsons, it is noteworthy that many African societies inherently accept the concept of an underlying unity among the myriad possible aspects of reality; yet ultimately all are part of a single entity. Interestingly, it was the South African statesman, Field Marshal Jan Smuts, from a Dutch-African lineage, who became a leading proponent of the concept of 'holism' – an indication that European diaspora in Africa has 'gone native' (like African diaspora in Europe). This contends that all things are part of a greater entity or 'whole' and according to many he was influenced by his 'holistic' theory when he drafted the Preamble to the United Nations Charter in 1945 which is a significant, but overlooked, African contribution to a global consciousness and policy.

Everywhere in the world, geography and climate influence social structures, and so they did influence the complexity of African societies in pre-colonial times. Population density was very low and distances between them were very wide. Nevertheless, there was a particularly rich legacy of interacting contacts between societies at both local and international levels. There are many theories elaborating on the biased perceptions Europeans developed regarding other societies in Asia and, perhaps especially, in Africa. This bias is a fundamental factor in the variety of 'Orientalism' that Edward Said wrote about, and a main source of their nowadays mostly hidden condescendence. British anthropologist Jack Goody has outlined the factors influencing such biased perceptions in Europe, or the West to take a broader context. In his book 'The East in the West' he writes about how many Europeans, including historians and theorists, have traditionally seen the societies of the East as 'static' or 'backward'. He has challenged this bias and pointed out how incorrect Western perceptions result from the application of Western criteria to societies using completely different standards of behaviour. It follows that someone from one society who attempts to judge the value of something from a society operating within a different paradigm must use the other's criteria or at least adjust their own to some extent and be aware of the variables being applied.

As in all societies, there are certain basic structures in African social systems. As people coexist and interact in society, they develop codes of conduct and frameworks to guide their societal positioning (status—leader/follower, parent/child, etc.) and the expectations (roles) attached to each person's position. Social structures refer to the formal organisation of status and roles that emerge from the actions of individuals or are deliberately introduced to guide how people fit into, coexist and interact in society. These structures define the roles (including their different functions, meanings and/or purposes) that accrue to everyone within a designated group (like family units, communities, corporate organisations, educational institutions, etc.) in society. These elements and groups not only determine and explain the development and functioning of modern social structures. They are also useful for understanding pre-colonial social structures and their inherent hierarchies/status, roles, relationships and interactions and their lasting influence on post-colonial conditions.

We explore these social stratifications as they exist in African societies by first looking at how the people and basic features of society such as families and clans are structured through the communitarian values system, and their evolution into more sophisticated kingdoms and city-states before exploring the social structures of the ruling or political class higher up the social strata.

Communitarianism as a Basis for African Social Values

African humanism is founded on the common notion of 'virtuous personhood'. This foundation sees human needs and interests as fundamental hence placing a great deal of emphasis on human welfare. This doctrine is held together within a strong sense of community also called communitarianism as earlier mentioned. It is the type of communitarianism that gave rise to African proverbs such as—'It takes a whole village to raise a child', implying that any child born into an African community is the collective responsibility of the entire village and not just the parents alone. For instance, a proverb of the Igala people (a tribe in the middle belt of what is modern-day Nigeria) says *'ko kma defu ichei iye, iye fubi imudeyi ja'*, meaning 'a child in the womb belongs to the mother, after birth, it belongs to the society. It further informs the value placed on human connectedness as another Igala proverb says 'Anone tanokole' meaning 'wealthiness in human resources is greater than material wealth'. In addition, the use of collective nouns such as 'we', 'our', 'us' and so on is typical of everyday language in most African countries such as 'our wife' or 'our husband'. These imply when a person marries, they marry not only into the immediate family of their partner but also into the local community where they come from.

This communitarianism is often referred to as the collectivist culture according to Geert Hofstede's cultural typology, but this is again a transposition of a modern Western concept into a different context. Communitarianism existed in Europe to some extent before the advent of market economies in the form of the commons. The peaceful coexistence and welfare of others have always been considered vital to the sustenance of African societies which informs fundamental values that bound pre-colonial indigenous African society together such as the ethical values of compassion, solidarity, reciprocity, cooperation, interdependence, hospitality, the primacy of the person, respect for life, sense of the sacred, familyhood, brotherhood, solidarity and social well-being. These are counted among the principles of the communalistic life of an African person, that primarily impose duties on the individual with respect to the community and its members. In this setup, moral duties trump rights hence, performing one's duties are underpinned by an awareness of needs rather than rights such that the fulfilling of duties to others is informed by needs and not because of their rights.

This understanding had a strong bearing on the notion of character and moral personhood within indigenous African communities. For instance, questions such as 'how should I live?' and 'what kind of person should I be?' were collectively understood by concepts such as the '*Omoluabi*' (virtuous person) concept in the Yoruba tradition, literally translated as the one 'who is born by the master of character'. Such an individual is often seen as excellence personified in both conduct and character typifying qualities such as '*iwa rere*' (good character), '*iwa pele*' (gentleness) and '*iwa irele*' (humility/respect). These individual level virtues formed the character foundation upon which communities and communal-level values systems were built resulting in systems such as 'team spirit' of Udama among the Igala people of Nigeria or '*Utu*' among the Kenyans and '*Umunthu*' in Malawi.

Central to all these notions is humaneness or being considerate, without which an individual is equated with an animal. For instance in Chichewa language of modern-day Malawi and Zimbabwe the saying

'*Kali kokha nkanyama, tili awiri ntiwanthu*' means 'when you are on your own you are as good as an animal of the wild; when there are two of you, you form a community'. On another hand, the notion of community transcends one's immediate community to accommodate people from other communities because we all descend from a common origin—God or as seen through the lenses of some of the indigenous religious systems—the pantheon of gods.

FAMILIES AND CLANS AS BASIC UNITS OF AFRICAN SOCIETIES

Archaeological evidence makes it clear that Africa has always been self-contained and self-sufficient, due to its vast space and limited population at these times. People lived in a web of ecological relationships; generation succeeding generation, like knots in a string, as elsewhere in pre-modern times. While populations were dispersed, varied in nature and disposition, some even antagonistic to one another, they generally shared an unbroken history and bond with their environment. This was an important factor that influenced where people congregated as societies, how they interacted and the roles they played. For example, not only did people form societies around sources of sustenance (food and drink), but the need for sustenance also formed the basis of Africans' earliest enterprise, hunting and gathering, as it did for all humans. In this way, the environment influenced where societies were formed, what people did and even who did what—men hunted, while women gathered.

The family has been unambiguously recognised as both the foundation and basic unit of every society. While a family is generally made up of the processes of blood relations, adoption, and socially sanctioned sexual unions between adults (including polygamous unions which were not uncommon) would typically constitute a wider relationship than those characteristic in Western, nuclear families. African families generally extend to cousins, grandparents, aunts, uncles, and other extended relatives of families. Additionally, the notion of the African family, depending on the place and context, often extends to include non-blood relations who become family by essence through their close bonds with another family. Hence, beyond biological links, family lineages and genealogical linkages are sociological as well. This implies that lineage and kinship can be edited or modified as necessary to accommodate other people. People can be inserted, or even insert themselves into certain lineages, often symbolically, albeit in a very meaningful and effective way. Thus, while families expand through the traditional means of marriage and birth, it is quite commonplace for close friendship to mature into 'family', or a friend to be named, regarded and treated as family in acknowledgement of the length of friendship and levels of closeness, trust and reliability felt. It is through this expansion that families link into the broader community which is the central core around which societies revolve. Consequently, the extended family was a necessary way of survival at a time when the political institution or power did not provide the security of the modern state. In Europe, the formation of a sovereign state fast-tracked development which de-emphasised the reliance on families for support.

As the basic unit of society, the family exemplifies the definition of status and roles in African social structures as each member of the family is assigned roles in accordance with their status: parents, children, extended family and friends turned family. However, in most cases, obligations to wider kin vary with time and are typically more widely invoked during times of crises, or during certain life-cycle events such as funerals. This remains a common practice in extended families on the continent, despite social change. Above all, the notion of ubuntu is interwoven with the understanding of family in the African context where the protection and advancement of the family name, values and expectations take precedence over individual interests.

Thus, the family serves as the foundation for and represents the values and codes of conduct of ubuntu and communitarianism in social interaction, exposing people to social and personal values. These values and codes are imposed on impressionable minds from a young age and handed down from one generation to the next. They are learned from, and begin to be enacted within, the family before being manifested in the community. In this way the family unit, being a microcosm of the broader society and community, shapes individuals for participation in society from an early age. It is from the family unit that individuals learn the values and principles of inclusion, interaction and society's expectations. The extension of family status beyond nuclear, blood or biological relations shows how very inclusive the African family system can be. And this models the broader, inclusive nature and type of African communities, creating a family-like lens through which relationships are interpreted and several social actors are included.

The African family not only functions as a locus for social inclusion, but it is also an institution for mutual help, reciprocity and nurturing and thus models the values of inclusivity and communitarianism of ubuntu. However, the criteria for inclusion in the family unit—blood and sociological relationships—also make for exclusion where the interests of in-groups are pursued over and beyond that of out-groups. This is replicated at the community/societal level too. For instance, in precolonial Africa, the imperatives of participating in the benefits accruing to large communities affected people at every level of society. However, being considered to 'belong' is necessary for participation. Belonging was attained by birth or family, or by other means such as through immigration, purchase or capture of other people as well as adoption in the case of destitute and orphans. All members of the community benefitted from the security of numbers and while most communities would prefer that outsiders do not join them, if need be, the new arrivals must be assimilated as quickly as possible, into the community.

From Clans to City-States: The Evolution of African Societies

A hierarchical structure for social interaction was the natural state of premodern societies. These structures became increasingly sophisticated as societies evolved. Hunting and gathering is the founding social structure (and economy) on which human society is based. It is the first and oldest form of society and still exists in some parts of Africa, even after one hundred thousand years. Hunter-gather societies were groups of people who formed clans and survived by continuously travelling in search of food and better living conditions. They settled where conditions were favourable and relied on the abundance of natural resources to survive, moving to the next favourable space when natural resources became unavailable. In these societies, women gathered and men hunted. Both often made contributions to the nourishment of the group, but women tended to make the greater contribution since they always returned with food from their foraging while men may at times go on for days without bringing any food home. Interestingly, the analysis of daily activities leaves little doubt as to which sex made the greater contribution to the overall nourishment of the group. When men went hunting, they came back empty-handed four times out of five, while women always returned from a foraging trip with something to eat. As Africa developed, hunter-gather societies reduced drastically as many preferred to live in one place with their families, start and lead a settlement community and indulge in trade and businesses that would amass wealth.

As families expanded and settled into the community with other expanding families, many of them began to rely on the wisdom of elders from which an age-grade system of community interaction emerged. In these gerontocratic and age-grade societies, major communal decisions were made in meetings of all the eligible adults with elders and household heads (chiefs) tended to have the greatest authority. The weight of a chief's opinion was measured by the multiple criteria of age, wealth and ability; status without ability was acknowledged, but not greatly respected.

While wealth was important, the age-grade system was crucial to the emergence of new decision-making elders in the community as it was a means of testing the ability and wisdom of future leaders. The age-grade system divided all males into groups using set criteria with each group getting allocated a standard set of duties (combined social and political duties). These duties changed as individuals grow through the years until those surviving accomplished all set duties. This resulted in the emergence of individuals with specific leadership qualities and astute judgements in each age group, whose capabilities were only exercised with the approval of their respective age groups and not by individual rights in what was some form of democracy. As some of these individuals act effectively, demonstrating sound reasoning as they advanced into senior age groups, they became highly respectable with the wise men status whose judgements were universally respected and acknowledged. Many of these kinds of societies still exist informally in different forms across Africa.

As these settled communities began to evolve into bigger towns and cities, a more sophisticated system of hierarchy emerged to form a different yet typical social structure. The emergent system were societies that organised themselves around social classes and hierarchies—leaders, merchants, religious leaders, labourers, free citizens and slaves. In most cases, those who discovered the settlement or community became the leaders of those settlements and their descendants maintained this position as the years go by. This, of course, was a consequence of the priority for the inclusion of family relations over outsiders.

These societies also appointed religious leaders, who were considered important by divine intervention. The wealthy of these societies were merchants who typically included successful traders, farmers and businessmen. Their wealth made them important and influential societal figures who had a say in the decisions made by leaders. For their part, free citizens were the ordinary people in the community who did not depend on anyone to survive and lived middle-class lives. As must be expected, slaves and laborers were the least respected in society and depended on their owners, usually the traders and merchants to survive. They are seen as belonging to, rather than in, the community.

Kingdoms and empires, the earliest formally structured political order, also evolved from the settlement of communities, especially those that indulged primarily in trade and business to amass wealth. They were a mixture of settled hunters and gatherers and social-class societies under the rulership of a monarchy within defined land territories. The richest individual was often quite likely the monarch who lived a grand lifestyle relative to everyone else or the individual to whom a significant proportion of local people (wives, children, kinsmen, friends, in-laws and the indebted) owed loyalty and to whom they paid tribute. It was usually this individual with whom international traders had the most contact and his regal behaviour doubtless imposed an obligation of careful formality if not obeisance upon locals and foreigners (including trans-Atlantic and Saharan foreigners) wishing to trade with him. It was also very common for monarchs to place family relations in charge of key/strategic aspects of the kingdom and only the family (most often first sons) inherited the title, properties and responsibilities of the king.

These societies usually expanded through war and invasion, assimilating more cultures and diversity in social conduct and interaction. Their rise began the proper demarcation of Africa before European presence, with many of these kingdoms going on to develop their own languages and culture as they became distinct civilizations. By the fourth century, kingdoms and empires had become the most popular forms of social structures that existed in Africa.

Besides kingdoms and the development of governments, city-states began to rise. They were urban settlements/rural villages that came together to form smaller but independent states that gained independence from bigger kingdoms. These states were often started by breakaway royals or merchants who were exiled or left due to issues they had with their original kingdoms. Others were formed from the attraction of fertile land (agriculture), mining, trade opportunities and logistical support (similar to Europe). As breakaway kingdoms, city-states usually mirrored the social interactions, hierarchies and relationships of their original kingdoms. However, while city-states enjoyed rapid development as a result of their trading activities, they were, most of the time, unable to last long as a kingdom since they were destroyed or absorbed into bigger kingdoms due to the absence of strong military protection.

Common across these societies was the benefit of belonging to and promoting the interests of certain groups (be it family, tribe, social class, or kingdom) over others and the subsequent expansion of social groups to accommodate their increase in strength, population or influence. In this way, core values associated with the family unit (like communitarianism) were manifested across every facet of societies, no matter how large they got, but also in the breakaway groups/cities that got formed.

African Pre-Colonial Socio-Political Structures and Systems

At the very top of the hierarchical society was the royal class typically comprising of ruling families which usually were communitarian themselves to preserve the ruling power of the family. These political structures which were supported by the social structures were, as in all such cases in other societies, very important in shaping not only the morphology of the society but also its economic activities which always underpin key aspects of a society's strength and resilience. As with the social structures above, the African political structure discussed here focusses primarily on sub-Saharan Africa.

In this region, from the time of early Africa-Europe interaction, one of the aspects noted by the Europeans was the egalitarian nature of African society. This often reinforced the European impression that African societies were undeveloped and simplistic, yet the reality was that of a deep, structural complexity coexisting with many simplistic elements in African political systems as in many other facets of African culture. Such realities are apparently still not fully understood by many Europeans in cultural interchanges with Africans and are among the ongoing challenges which prevent full potential from being achieved in the relationship between both continents.

The political administration of pre-colonial, social formations in Africa, for the most part, fell into two main categories: small societies without formally specialised or institutionalised political roles or structures for administering executive, legislative or judicial functions commonly referred to as stateless societies; and territorial states with formally centralised government administrations and hierarchical organisation like the Zulu of Southern Africa, the Songhai of West Africa, the Luba kingdom in Central Africa and the kingdoms of Buganda and Ankole in East Africa.

There were, of course, societies—tribes and chiefdoms—with political institutions that were not firmly situated in either category. For the most part, they did not have (enough) political centralisation to fit into either category. It is important to note that as degrading as 'being stateless' may sound, it neither connotes being disintegrated nor lacking defined structures for administering executive, legislative or judicial functions. It simply means that these functions were decentralised and spread across kinship, clan and tribal groups within larger communal groups. And the norms and rules of behaviour and actions towards others were maintained largely by consensus.

Decentralisation, therefore, offered stateless societies an instituted system of checks and balances in which two or more power centres across all societal levels were balanced against each other so that no single centre predominated over the others. It also offered a greater degree of freedom and autonomy, especially to smaller/marginalised groups as according to the US' Thomas Jefferson, societies that live without government enjoy in their general mass an infinitely greater degree of freedom and happiness. Stateless societies were characteristic of the foremost hunter-gatherer and gerontocratic societies, especially in West Africa, before the expansion of African societies and the need for transformation led to the migration and emergence of more centralised political practices.

The move from decentralisation to centralisation was, of course, not abrupt. As societies evolved, their political institutions remained in flux and evolved in parallel. Evolution followed from interaction with other African and non-African societies through trade, religion, etc. and as societies expanded their territorial boundaries through military conquest, the peaceful assimilation of other societies, consensual amalgamation of different societies, etc. Change in political structures was also propelled by local and regional struggles to control resources, trade and political authority. As mentioned earlier, the expansion of families into communities led to the reliance on chiefs for decision-making and leadership. More political authority rested on the chief(s) whose wealth and status secured the allegiance and tributes (in labour and in kind) of those who received the right to land and settle; on the person who held social seniority in the dominant ruling line of descent; or in some instances, the person who had religious or sacred authority over others like in the case of Usman dan Fodio who founded the Sokoto Caliphate in 1804 in West Africa as was described in the first chapter of this publication.

The further expansion of these societies through consolidation and the subsequent conquest or voluntary incorporation by a strong chiefdom of multiple subordinate chiefdoms (like the Ashanti kingdom that had emerged from the Akan clan-based chiefdoms around Kumasi in today's Ghana and the important Dahomey kingdom in today's Benin) required further evolution of the accompanying political institutions and practices. Through multiple layers of authority, it had to be possible to coordinate the symbolic submission and payment of tributes and taxes. And there were also the administrative, economic and military structures required to support its expansion. These structures were primarily needed to control access to resources such as water and other natural resources as well as to manage equitable land holding, trade and law enforcement. Appointed officials could settle disputes executive punishments and make judicial determinations.

At times, these authorities functioned at varying levels. At the family level, for example, the head of a clan or lineage, who is usually the most senior male member retained the rights to execute these functions for members of the family or their clan. Existential threats to going concerns also required security structures to protect the social order. This would range from small-scale militia to larger military and complex military institutions and alliances needed to neutralise the threats of small-scale cattle raiders, wars launched by other chiefdoms or kingdoms, or outsiders such as the Europeans. And as mentioned in Chapter 1, military conquest resulted in the institutionalisation of slavery and a slave trade, which in some places became central to the economic and political functioning of the kingdom.

The hierarchical formation of these structures and the ways in which roles were allocated to each function was also a reflection of the social dynamics of kinship and communitarianism that is integral to African societies. And this took place in combination with the distinct cultures, demography, geographical terrain, religious beliefs and interaction with the world outside the particular society concerned, among other things. So, while monarchies were quite common, the choice of monarchs, even when restricted to kinsfolk of the monarchs, required a selection process that involved the representation of the whole community.

For instance, the Bunyoro in present-day Uganda and the kings of the Kongo Kingdom were chosen from among numerous eligible descendants of the previous monarch. For Kongo, since any descendent was eligible, the pool of possible claimants became large over time and an 'electoral college' system comprising a council (about nine to twelve individuals) was created to choose the new Manikongo. In some cases, like the Luba, (located largely in southern-central, present-day DRC), the only eligible claimants to the kingship were those who descended from either of two families, the Kongolo or Kalala Ilunga who were believed to possess a sacred quality which was only vested in the blood of kin and transmissible only through males.

The social dynamics of kinship and communitarianism were also integral to the way the kingdoms were governed. The Bunyoro monarch, the Mukama, for instance, was assisted in governing by a brother of the former king, the Olewiri and both were supported by palace officials, advisers, retainers, important chiefs and honoured 'crown-weavers' who were selected by the Mukama to perform various governing functions under the Mukama's authority. Similarly, the Buganda kingdom (located in modern-day Uganda) whose rulers were of the same dynasty as the Bunyoro kingdom, also had a complex system of governing institutions. Its chiefs, the Batongole, were appointed by the king, (Kabaka), as governing officials, for the most part, to centralise political and military power and suppress the authority of subordinated chiefs.

The highest governing body for Buganda was, however, the council, the Lukiko, which shared responsibility with the Kabaka for the appointment of sub-chiefs, including senior and district chiefs. The most senior of these chiefs, the Katikiro, served as prime minister and chief justice. He handled all state matters and cases and referred the ones that had his decisions challenged to the Kabaka. There was also the Kimbugwe who was entrusted with the Kabaka's umbilical cord and oversaw all the religious and cult matters relating to the royal family. The district chiefs were tasked with the collection of tributes and the adjudication of cases, wielding authority in their own districts over the sub-chiefs who were also appointed by the Kabaka. Some district chiefs served as governors over tributary chiefdoms.

The king's mother, also known as the Namasole, was usually very influential with powers over her own jurisdictions which was complete with estates and personal court. The Buganda queen, the Lubuga, was the sister of the king by another mother and, often had the power of making key appointments in addition to having powers over her own estates. Dispute resolution was also a key responsibility of the Lubuga. As would be expected Princes and princesses, known as the balangira and bambejja respectively, born into the family and held titles. They are both given their own estates in districts which they had to administrate themselves by appointing titled chiefs to help supervision of their interests. Royal family daughters could get elevated to the status of royal men but were required to relinquish the rights to marriage and child-bearing, by becoming virtually genderless, as a means to restrict the number of potential heirs in the royal line of descent.

Even kingdoms like the Luba, whose monarchs held absolute authority, had administrative structures that reflected the dynamics of kinship and communitarianism through the role of chiefs and other titleholders. The Luba's hierarchical, political structure rested on lineage-based homesteads, villages under headmen, chiefdoms each under a territorial chief, the Kilolo and provinces. The sacred quality of the Luba monarchs gave them the divine right and accompanying supernatural powers to rule and challenges to the king could only come from other descendants of these two rulers. The titleholders were usually relatives of the king and when the king died, they were replaced by relatives of the new king. The Luba Kingdom had two key practices that sustained it: perpetual succession and positional kinship. Successors took the name and office of the original office holder, hence all rulers had the same name even though they may not necessarily be related by blood.

In the Mutapa empire of what is now Zimbabwe, for instance, each village had a village head who received counsel from the collective of all adult men at the village meeting place. At a higher level is a system of collective governance through a ward system called the 'dunhu'. This comprised multiple villages governed by a ward chief, 'sadunhu', usually headquartered in a town where a more formal and selected men met at the ward. Sadunhus were usually selected by their ward, mostly through succession and confirmed at the next level of authority, that of the chiefs or 'madzishe'. Each madzishe was headquartered at a muzinda, the capital of their chiefdom and the council of madzishe only selected men either from the ruling family or commoners known for their exceptional wisdom or talents. The council also served as the highest court of appeal for the chiefdom. Similarly, the emperor Mwenemutapa, also ruled with a council composed of the governor of the provinces, known as the Nengomasha, the chief minister or Nevinga, the captain of the armies, the Mukomohasha and other appointed officials. The decisions made by the ruling

Mwenemutapa were usually subject to the authority of spiritual leaders who were spirit mediums.

Some societies, however, like the Igbo, in present-day eastern Nigeria, chose to remain stateless, without the multi-layered, political structuring that other kingdoms had evolved to. This was neither a reflection of stagnancy nor a lack of evolution or adaptation by the Igbos, but a rejection of autocratic governance. The Igbo had a democratic, political structure that encouraged communal participation in decision-making through village assemblies and decisions based on popular consensus. Igbos kinship-based structures were common at the levels of a compound with an extended family, a cluster of lineage-based segments and villages within which governing functions were also performed by age grades, associations, cults and priests.

However, monarchical institutions were adopted from external influences credited to the Benin or Igala kingdoms in West Africa, and these were reflected in the structured hierarchy of titled chiefs subordinate to a head chief called the 'Obi' or 'Eze'. While some villages managed, at some point, to blend democracy with monarchy and aristocracy, generally, the monarchy faced extinction most likely as a result of the tyranny and absoluteness of the throne's occupant, with many electing against having a centralised authority. The rejection of the monarchy, which appears to have given rise to the concepts of 'Ezebuilo', i.e. 'the king is the enemy', and 'enwe Eze', i.e. 'the Igbo have no kings', led to the combination of democracy, gerontocracy and aristocracy for which the Igbos of modern-day Nigeria are known. This suggests that, like other African societies, the political institutions of the Igbos were fluid, adapting to the needs and especially the voice of the Igbo people. However, in the second half of the nineteenth century another crisis resulting from the then-European encroachment on the Niger River and the military aggression of the British Royal Niger Company, threw up a natural leader, Onyekomeli Idigo, who founded a royal dynasty which has endured to this day.

It is important to mention that women played major roles in the political framework of pre-colonial African kingdoms. While positions of public office were predominantly occupied by men, women also held public political and judicial positions in various African kingdoms. African pre-colonial political history is incomplete without the political, judicial, diplomatic and military leadership and exploits of renowned queens. This included Makeda of Ethiopia (known as the Queen of Sheba, tenth century BC), Dido of Carthage (first century BC), Cleopatra of Egypt (reigned 51–30 BC), Amanirenas of Kush (reigned 40–10 BC), Gudit of Aksum (960–1001 AD), Amina of Zazzau (present-day Zaria in northern Nigeria; reigned 1576–1610 AD), Nzinga of Ndogo and Matamba (in modern-day Angola, reigned 1624–1663 AD) and the Rain Queens of the Balobedu (of the Limpopo Province of South Africa), to name but a few. The social and religious influence of queen consorts and queen mothers like Nefertiti of Egypt (1370–1330 BC) and Nandi of the Zulu (the mother of King Shaka. 1760–1827 AD) should not be forgotten either.

In various African societies, queen mothers have been influential in the governance of kingdoms either through the influence they had on their sons (like Nandi of the Zulu) or ruling alongside their sons like the AmaSwazi of Southern Africa where the Swazi king shared authority with his mother. The king remained the highest judicial authority and commander-in-chief of the armed forces, but the queen mother held a prominent role usually with their own royal jurisdiction which included the second highest court complete with counsellors and regiments commanded by royal princes. The titled queen of Bungada, in addition to having her own estates, adjudicated disputes and was empowered to appoint chiefs. And in some African kingdoms like Lunda in Central Africa and Ashanti in modern-day Ghana, perpetual succession to the throne as well as positional kinship and inheritance was recognised under a matrilineal kinship organisation. Queen mothers also commonly served as regents during the minority of the heir following the death of rulers or exile of their kin like with Yaa Asantewaa of the Ashanti. Thus, while women have been the primary influences for shaping social interactions through the family unit, they have also been influential in the political formation, administration and advancement of African states.

Colonisation and African Socio-Political Structures

The colonisation of African regions, without a doubt, influenced the existing social structures on the continent. As noted, while core elements of communitarianism remained, prior to colonisation, the structures of status, roles, interactions and relationships were already evolving as groups expanded and migrated. And this evolution continued as Africans interacted with colonial masters who, as expected, also attempted to impose new forms of social structure through governance, religion and economic activities, albeit with limited success. What happened instead was that Africans evolved, adapting their social structures to the demands of both the colonial and post-colonial eras, which in turn led to the emergence of new social formations. These started as traditional, pre-colonial, institutions and became transformed to operate in new contexts with new symbols and meanings thereby widening the sociocultural systems and frameworks. Colonialism fractured the moral and social order which formerly preserved the pre-colonial indigenous institutions as they sought anchors in the changed milieu.

While colonialism influenced the retardation of some social structures, it also offered others an unprecedented growth opportunity. In many cases, this was especially relevant for political structures given that the need for better conformity and synchronisation with European/Western structures of governance often demanded the creation of such new structures in African societies. In other cases, even if the demand was not there, the new social context allowed new structures and practices, often not fully synchronised with traditional norms, for politically related matters as much or in some cases even more, than for others. Such transformations were across all parts of society, having considerable relevance for the functioning and in many cases stability, of African societies in the post-colonial world. The transformation of political systems had especially important implications for stable, responsible, good governance according to any established criteria in post-colonial Africa especially with many traditional formats being transmuted as noted above.

There are many illustrative examples among others that in pre-colonial societies, certain symbols were reserved for those custodians of order whose responsibility was to keep the tradition of their societies. Elders and monarchs often took on this role. It is possible, especially with reference to nobility, that such symbols (like elaborate and distinctive dresses and adornments, facial marks, polygamy, and even such items as the umbrella) were strictly reserved for the upper echelon of society as a way of distinguishing themselves from the rest of society. Any attempts to appropriate these symbols by other groups could be punished. However, with colonialism, there was a dramatic change and these restricted symbols of culture became substantiated and generalised to all members of the distinct groups that were fighting for their separate place in the new order. Whereas in pre-colonial Africa the use of these symbols could be punished, in post-colonial Africa their use by the general public is rewarded with group approval. Thus, modern forms of traditional attire for example, which were royal or chieftain in origin, have spread to all levels of society with the help of the generalisation which colonialism promoted.

Another post-colonial, social formation consists of migrated social structures and constructs which in many cases appear to be transported from the West to Asia and Africa and transplanted into the new colonial systems. Examples of such constructs include those of democracy and the rule of law with its peculiar, Western connotations; institutions such as universities and national statehood; bureaucratic establishments and parliaments. These were models brought into colonies wholesale from Europe. While the previously highlighted formation represented an emergence from within Africa, this represented an expansion of European institutions to Africa, but readapted with acquired textures and variations that make them peculiarly African. The consequence of this is the (somewhat imposed) inheritance of social structures from Europe without the underlying cultural, moral and ethical foundations that support the self-sustained refinement and expansion of these structures. The evidence of this is an infusion (that frequently leads to a clash) of elements that are core to indigenous, African, social structures (like the prioritisation of the family unit and communitarianism, African social hierarchies, etc.) into imported institutions (like universities, civil service, hospitals, etc.), disembodying their original, moral contents and implicating ethics.

Finally, there are emergent social structures that are neither indigenous to Africa nor brought from outside but have developed in the post-colonial environment to fill gaps and needs that indigenous social and imported social structures could not fulfil in the new reality. These emergent structures have analogies in the West and elsewhere, they have a logic of their own and are very peculiar with distinct political and sociological structures. Unlike the social formations presented earlier, emergent social structures are difficult to discern because they are very often consciously smeared with tradition or modernity to give them the appearance of ultra-tradition or modernity. Also, while indigenous and imported social structures represent formal aspects of situations before, during and after colonialism, the emergent social structures represent informal elements of colonialism.

Tribalism in West Africa presents an example of emergent social structures. Tribes, which were usually autonomous with their own values and moral systems as well as well-defined geographical boundaries were dislocated by the forces of colonialism because tribes were incompatible with the new, widened, integrated existence of colonialism. Tribalism emerged under the aegis of this disruptive system of colonialism. It is a construct that defines a model of behaviour that is unacceptable in post-colonial, ethnic relationships. It has a linkage with tribes, not because tribes exist anymore but because the acts that constitute tribalism have the atavistic aura of (exclusion-oriented) behaviours which are considered appropriate for a past form of existence in the tribal setting, but which are deemed destructive in polyethnic systems of social life.

A tribalist is a non-tribesman who exhibits anti-social behaviour in a non-tribal setting in such a way as to threaten the new forms of existence with reversion to a past form of restricted, tribal, social organisation. Tribalism is not only unique to modern, post-colonial Africa and perhaps Asia, but it was in fact generated in the re-organisations and re-orderings that were provoked in colonialism. Thus, tribalism as a social phenomenon is neither indigenous to Africa nor imported through colonialism.

Additionally, emergent social structures are evident in the intrinsic combination of indigenous and imported formations in post-colonial, African, social interactions. It is nearly impossible, in any prolonged social interaction with Africans, to miss the fusion of distinctly Western social elements with distinctly African elements. A good example of this is how Africans fuse local dialects with the English language so perfectly that it comes across as a language of its own. Another is the respect afforded to elders and hierarchies that is extended to imported, Western, professional institutions where respect is expected and balanced between professional hierarchies (irrespective of age) and older age brackets at the same time. More importantly, however, despite the evolution and adaptations of African social structures over time, the role of the family as the basic unit of society and crux of social interaction and the values and codes of conduct of ubuntu and communitarianism, remain at the heart of African social structures and interaction.

Implications for African Values Systems

As earlier discussed, with colonisation it is not strange to have colonised nations subjugated to learning the norms, cultures, beliefs, religion and traditions of their colonisers. This reality does not imply the extinction of the traditional values of the colonised nation. For Africa, the impact of colonisation in introducing new ways of organising societies and in the creation of new social orders did not completely eradicate pre-colonial social systems. The nature of this challenge takes its root from the complexities the African context presents such that Africa has two nominal contexts—the modern and traditional. The modern context is typically associated with Western civilisation and values concentrated in the urban areas of most countries.

The traditional context is however represented by traditional rulers, chiefs and council of elders which used to be in the rural areas but now due to urbanisation, also exist in urban towns and cities. The roots of this traditional context are traceable to the pre-colonial African societies which were known for their well-defined norm and values. These norms and values would underpin rituals, tacit contracts, human relations as well as inter-kingdom diplomatic relations. Moreover, ethnic and tribal identities as well as communal and family links typify the nature of social interactions in the traditional contexts. As social orders became increasingly sophisticated, these values and norms became more entrenched in the consciousness of the African mind, thereby forging belief systems we call traditions. In referring to the 'African mind' care must be taken not to assume that African is a country nor should it be assumed that the norms and values are necessarily homogenous.

These two contexts come with different economic activities, institutional, psychological and social-cultural systems which at times coexist peacefully or in conflict thereby affecting how states, processes and activities function. Also, the complexities of African societies till date are inherent in the heterogeneity of the peoples of the continent such that today, over 16 languages are spoken in Egypt, 250 in Nigeria, 70 in Kenya and more than 12 in South Africa. The ethnic groups speaking these different languages have their own customs and beliefs which may be shared to a large extent with other groups within the same geographic boundaries and beyond but will still have their own nuances that distinguish them. Hence, this chapter acknowledges the heterogeneity of cultures and subcultures prevalent on the continent yet hopes to find a central thread that can speak to the continent as a whole given the shared African culture which has emerged over the centuries.

Bridging this identified traditional-modernity gap poses two traps along two extremes. First, is that individuals who were brought up in the modern context and are exposed to Western values can frame their value systems on the assumption that the modern context is an 'upgraded' version of an 'outdated' traditional system. Some post-colonialists argue this is the intended effect of colonialism in the first place. The problem with a values system embedded in this line of thinking is the tendency to disregard thoughts and ideas from the traditional context as primitive and incapable of being useful in resolving Africa's issues which can be conceptualised, rather ignorantly as essentially 'modern' issues. For instance, bright ideas originating from foreign countries at times struggle to work well in African contexts because they are not well adapted to suit the realities of say the rural communities. These ideas are therefore deemed irrelevant and incapable of addressing the issues faced in those parts of society.

Second is also the potential challenge of embracing the values of the traditional approach in rebellion against colonialism and its modern ideologies. This line of thinking assumes Africa's problem arose from the impact of colonialism and that Western values have little or no place in the governing of African societies. Leaders and indeed citizenry who hold on to this line of thinking are hard-core traditionalists whose position tends to assume Africa can be rescued from the 'invasion' of foreign cultures.

Again, this extreme position can be naïve and misinformed. In the largely globalised world we now live in, there are very few communities, mostly in very remote parts of the world that can claim no influence of any foreign culture on their polity. With this comes major shifts in societal values typified by technological advances, demographic shifts, shifts in global economic power, urbanisation, resource scarcity all of which have changed the expectations of the citizenry of their leaders. African citizens now have strong platforms and a voice like never before in our history as a people which was evident for instance in the Arab spring uprisings, and the opposition against African dictators in recent history. The better alternative is to bring together the best of both worlds.

Conclusions

In this chapter, we explored some of the well-known values that characterised historical indigenous African societies. Social behaviour, typical African values and hidden consciousness that shaped African societies are discussed. Special attention is given to the African tradition of communitarianism—a strong sense of community that is very typical of all African pre-colonial kingdoms and persists until today in shaping the individual-community interaction. Africans and Europeans alike could learn from how virtues and values in historical indigenous African societal contexts regulated behaviour and conduct. This is done with a view to advancing the argument that to forge the future collaboratively, we must appreciate systems that worked in the past and how insights from these systems can help shape the current realities of Africa's leadership and geopolitical landscape.

These said, African socio-political systems have undergone many changes because of the colonial process and in many ways continue to undergo transformation in the post-colonial era especially as it is one where they are not restricted by traditional norms as before. This is all especially true of sub-Saharan African societies which are those that the Europeans initially found to be very different from those with which they were used to dealing. In many ways, post-colonial African society contains more familiar elements for the Europeans, yet many basic differences still exist and the fragility along with the instability of many post-colonial African societies often continues to undermine a good comprehension of their African counterparts by the Europeans while in some cases old stereotype impressions of African inferiority seem to be further confirmed. The need for improved understanding that makes adjustments for variations between European and African societal paradigms, particularly by Europeans, is again apparent.

In drawing conclusions about how African socio-political systems have transformed in the post-colonial era, it can be noted that overall, for many kingdoms, the kinship political institutions that sufficed during the early stages of societal development became inadequate and African societies adapted and transformed into more centralised, hierarchical systems of government. The emerging political practices remained linked to and overlapped with, social, economic and religious institutions across the multiple, social groups incorporated, yet all were transmuted through colonial and ongoing post-colonial processes. This led to multiplicity. For example, religious authorities sometimes held political office, or wielded authority over political office, limiting the powers of governing officials. Furthermore, laws codified governance and politics enforced by chiefs in village courts. Governance was accomplished through intermediate levels of political authority and governance: counsellors, councils and subordinate chiefs; and political authority overlapped with the power and functions of social, military and religious leadership and authorities.

This overlap of political practices also meant that the political institutions in Africa were, for many kingdoms, a complex, multi-layered, consolidation of hierarchical roles and systems of government. Different societies had different flavours of gerontocracy combined with democracy and monarchy; others were imperialists but remained gerontocratic in many ways. There were great African dynasties, theocracies and feudalistic governments, just like in other parts of the world. And all of this complexity of governing institutions existed before the imposition of colonial European rule, which for the most part, disrupted indigenous political authority and practices. The pre-colonial governing institutions that were allowed to continue were severely restricted to meet the colonizers' goals.

The harsh reality of colonial rule was contrary to the political practices Africans were used to and failed to meet the criteria for legitimacy to rule the African people. The legitimacy of pre-colonial regimes was supported by wider consultations in governance processes and judicial proceedings. Even powerful rulers were still restrained by alternative authorities, usually religious authorities and councils and religious authorities. The institutions of governance were undergirded by the rule of law and religious beliefs which bound the ruler as well as his subjects. By definition, European colonial regimes are invasive and at best, foreign systems imposed by conquest and subjugation to enforce compliance. The rise of anticolonial movements forced colonial regimes to create new ways of legitimization by creating consultative channels and councils. These attempts belied the underlying colonial goals to maintain control and rule.

Though the new systems of governance and political institutions that were imposed on the Africans to shape their post-colonial future were not completely new to them, they were always different from their pre-colonial predecessors in significant ways. Similarities may be superficial, and they may be intrinsically different in ways that are not apparent. Nevertheless, the roots of African political systems in the social formations of kinship and communitarianism means that no matter what the political institutions look like, their practices remain shaped by the core constructs of African social philosophy like Ubuntu. So, as has historically been the case, contemporary African political institutions, rather than being replicas, are adaptations to the transitions of contemporary, post-colonial African realities, not quite the same as pre-colonial nor as Western systems. For instance, the common judicial function of customary courts and the role of various multicultural/traditional, cultural and political institutions exist alongside Western political institutions in many African countries. And while these adapted systems, which are based on the social principles of 'my kin/community first', may appear deficient, detrimental or even illegal from Western perspectives, they reflect the philosophy that guides African social formations: ubuntu, kinship and communitarianism. This, of course, is not an attempt to excuse the bad governance practices that have been detrimental to the advancement of both pre- and post-colonial Africa but to facilitate an understanding of the social formations on which African political institutions and systems are built.

CHAPTER 5

Colonialism and the Struggle for Independence

Introduction: The Twilight of the Colonial Period

Whereas in 1930 only Liberia and Ethiopia, or Abyssinia as it was then known, were independent, apart from South Africa that was ruled by its white minority without the indigenous peoples having equal rights, by the end of the twentieth century every single nation in Africa had gained its freedom after a long and arduous, often bloody struggle for political independence. Like most modern African countries, the colonial inheritance included the very geopolitical contours of the new state, with Ghana having been assembled from what had been the colonies of the Gold Coast and Ashanti, the protectorate of the Northern Territories and the British-mandated territory of western Togoland. The period of European colonisation in Africa had initially crept rather slowly into the mixture of relationships in the Africa-Europe interface from the late fifteenth century onwards. Yet in piecemeal fashion, it slowly gained pace until by the late nineteenth century there was what is often called 'the scramble for Africa'.

The Scramble for Africa, was the invasion, annexation, division and colonisation of most of Africa by seven western European powers during a short period known to historians as New Imperialism (between 1881 and 1914). Just 10% of Africa was under formal European control in 1870 which increased to 90% by 1914. Only two nations Ethiopia (Abyssinia) and Liberia remained independent states, though

© The Author(s), under exclusive license to Springer Nature Switzerland AG 2023
A. Adewale and S. Schepers, *Reimaging Africa*,
https://doi.org/10.1007/978-3-031-40360-6_5

Ethiopia would later be invaded and occupied by Italy in 1936. The Berlin Conference of 1884, where the seven Western powers met and divided Africa, is usually referred to as the starting point. There were considerable political rivalries among the European empires and countries in the last quarter of the nineteenth century, nevertheless, the final partitioning of Africa was done through diplomatic negotiation. Later in the nineteenth century, the European nations adopted to direct rule having transitioned from 'informal imperialism'—i.e. exercising military influence and economic dominance. This brought about colonial imperialism.

Early in the period of colonisation, the desire for independence gradually began to assert itself in almost every African country. In a relatively short time, the movement towards independence strengthened in intensity, to be met by varying levels of resistance by colonial authorities in what became known as the 'struggle' for independence. For the most part, this struggle for Africa's independence was a convergence of ideological, sociological, psychological and economic factors that influenced Africans' peaceful and violent agitation for self-rule well into the 1900s and can be traced to the continent's resistance to Europe's scramble for Africa.

Though communitarian in societal structure, Africans appreciated the need for personal freedoms and revolted against its infringement by Europeans. The resistance to colonial occupation began with spontaneous local uprisings. The Temne and Mende of modern-day Sierra Leone, for instance, revolted against the Hut Tax imposed by the British while the Nama and Herero people in what is now Namibia revolted against forced labour. Revolts were the only option as Europeans considered all good land as terra nullius and grabbed it at will. Violent revolts were, however, militarily unsuccessful due to the lack of a country-wide organisational base and they resulted in more brutal suppression by colonial powers. Following this, people adopted more moderate strategies, employing conventional means of activism and associations to address specific grievances.

The European response, however, was to thwart these reforms as they were loath to spend any money on 'natives' or share any of their power with Africans. In response, Africans ultimately began to consider self-rule as their only option. While African resistance was stirred up by the ideological uplift of African nationalism, the achievement of self-rule needed several catalytic factors to come together, including the experience of colonial oppression itself, the influence of missionaries and missionary education, the psychological and economic effects of the First and Second World Wars, the investment opportunities brought about by Europe's post-war economic boom, the platform for reform offered by the League of Nations/United Nations and the ideology of Pan-Africanism. All these factors interacted and provide an avenue for understanding not just the motivation, but also the process of Africa's struggle for independence.

The colonial period was a negative one for the Africa-Europe interface in many ways. But among the worst was the manner in which it helped entrench a new biased, patronising regard for Africans by the Europeans and embedded colonial economies which were purposefully slanted in the favour of the colonial powers. In the socio-ecosystems of the colonial period, there were positive factors for Africa such as European education and health care systems, yet the negative offsets remained substantial.

The French economist Thomas Piketty is among those who have clarified the inequalities which colonialism produced. Piketty identified two ages of European colonialism. The first was from 1500 to 1850, characterised by 'military domination and forced displacement and/or extermination of populations'. The second was from 1850 to the 1960s which he notes 'is often said to have been kinder and gentler' although 'violence was scarcely absent'. He, too, focussed on the ideologies that sustained forms of inequality within colonial societies as much as the economic results. Piketty said that there is an urgent need for greater economic equality in all global societies, bringing with it transformed societies that are both more just and more stable. These words would seem especially appropriate for the many inequalities in African societies which largely result from the colonial period.

African Nationalism in the Struggle for Independence

African nationalism refers to a group of political ideologies based on the idea of national self-determination and the political independence of the states created by the Europeans, often without taking into account historic, social and cultural background. Rather than seeing themselves as ethnic divisions (for example Kikuyu, Igbo, Zulu, etc.), nationalist leaders wanted Africans to view themselves as nation-states (Kenya, Nigeria, South Africa, etc.). In a way, it was the extension of communal kinship beyond and across ethnic units to include all ethnicities within the nation and even beyond the continent. In fact, the European Westphalian state concept.

According to political philosophers like Francis Fukuyama, ideal state-building requires overcoming the strong bonds of kin which only result in nepotism, dynasticism, tribalism and clannishness.

The extension of communal kinship beyond and across ethnic units was particularly important for nation-building and the nationalism it supported because Africa had been sliced into different colonies based on natural resources. This had been without any regard for historic kingdoms, ethnic groups, religions or languages, as European powers haggled and battered over gold mines and plantations, copper deposits and forests. It was as simple as drawing straight lines over territories and grouping them into colonies, pushing together ethnic groups that for centuries usually lived in different states, spoke different languages, worshipped different religions and had long histories of rivalry and suspicion, while at the same time separating ethnicities with shared identities.

The manner in which colonial borders thus divided up people is well illustrated in the following examples. The borders of modern Burkina Faso cut across territory that traditionally belonged to twenty-one different social, cultural and linguistic groups. The Ewe people who have a five-hundred-year history were split between Ghana and Togo. The Somali people were divided into French Somaliland, British Somalia, Italian Somalia, Ethiopian Somalia and the Somali region of northern Kenya. Historic Abyssinia (Ethiopia) was partitioned into Ethiopia, Eritrea and Djibouti and the Anyuaa and Nuer were split between Ethiopia and South Sudan. The few countries which were spared this partitioning and remained more homogenous, such as Botswana, would also be those whose political stability and economic growth would later surpass the average in Africa.

It was therefore important that organisations formed to protest colonial rule, depending on the territory allotted to a particular colonial power (like France, Britain or Germany) to share a common sense of motivation and purpose that was only possible from a transformed, unified identity. However, this appeared possible only to the extent of a shared sense of oppression by and desire for liberation from colonial powers. On the one hand, it was virtually impossible for Africans to organise on a nation-wide basis, so regional or ethnic organisations became the most practical option.

In their own interests, Europeans played ethnic groups and regions against one another and purported the resistance almost entirely in racial terms, characterising the more militant or outspoken ones as being antiwhite. For example, the Mau Mau Uprising (1952–1960) against British rule in Kenya was labelled by the Western media as an aimless, fanatically violent rebellion, bent on killing and maiming any white person for the fun of it. Such understanding was not only wrong but strengthened European racism. The goal of such an interpretation was to divorce the struggle from the legitimate grievances that undergirded it.

Despite these challenges, the desire for self-determination prevailed as Africans simply wanted their territories back and the freedom to live their lives as they saw fit. And they were willing to do whatever it took to achieve this, including defying the odds and unifying across ethnicities and even colonial territories. Their agitation for independence was further bolstered by a number of catalytic factors that not only fuelled a surge in African nationalism but also facilitated achieving independence. These included colonial oppression, missionary churches and education, World Wars I and II, Europe's golden age of economic growth in the 1950s and 60s, the League of Nations/United Nations and pan-Africanism ideology.

Colonial Oppression

While a few may have benefitted materially, colonisation was mostly a negative, exploitative and oppressive experience for the indigenous peoples. Africans were humiliated as second-class citizens, their culture denigrated and their land confiscated. They were not only faced with the brutality of the European military; European immigrants, who were encouraged (or forced) to relocate to Africa and given large tracts of land to farm (on large plantations established for growing cash crops for export), forced Africans to provide cheap labour with severe consequences for African communities.

Additionally, prior to colonisation, Africans were not alien to the experience of political freedom and consensual government (which the Europeans called democracy). As was described in Chapter 3 African societies were communitarian in which the needs and rights of communities as a whole took precedence over those of the individual. However, this did not equate to a lack of appreciation for personal freedoms. African communities usually consulted a great deal in an atmosphere of unfettered debate and discussion. The African palaver model is famous for its conflict resolution.

Chosen leaders were held accountable for their actions with those who resist the wishes and demands of their people were often overthrown or replaced. Even with monarchical governments/hereditary systems, the hereditary rule was permitted only as long as leaders functioned within the permissive requirements of acceptable service agreed upon by their communities. When a leader was incompetent or betrayed the people's trust by being unfair or cruel, he was voted out and another leader was chosen from a different house or family. Thus, familiarity with political systems that were accountable to the people made colonial oppression all the more frustrating for Africans and stoked the fire of their struggle for independence.

Missionary Churches and Education

In most African colonies, Christian missionaries came either before the colonial takeovers or after the declaration of a colony. This was, however, not the advent of Christianity in Africa, Christianity's foray into Africa goes back to Roman times, when Mark the Evangelist founded the Coptic Orthodox Church in Alexandria. The Portuguese then introduced the Catholic Church to Africa in the late 1400s in Benin and was soon extended to Congo and Angola.

For the most part, however, by educating Africans, the missionaries unintentionally provided a platform to demand independence. The church provided a pacifying effect on the African people, with its emphasis on spiritual matters over earthly affairs. The church also served to provide spiritual solace and succour to disintegrating African communities hit hard by colonial policy, although usually without attacking the root causes. For example, after the defeat of the Maji Maji rebellion (1905–1907) where the Tanzanians chose to resist oppressive German colonialism, Christianity offered spiritual encouragement to the Africans who due to the devastating defeat (around 120,000 Africans were killed) had lost faith in their ancestral spirits.

Perhaps most importantly, missionaries brought Western education usually in the form of mission schools which were the main educational institutions. The administrative and operational costs of educating were often borne entirely by the missions. In some cases, the central colonial government provided some funding while the missions were left with the responsibility of staffing and curriculum development. Mission education had three goals: to provide basic literacy to enable Christian education and training; to impart Western values, without which the missionaries believed Africans could not progress; to raise the productivity of African workers, without necessarily empowering them sufficiently so as to challenge colonial rule.

However, the purposes of missionary churches in Africa had dual consequences. While they appeared to propagate the European colonisation agenda, they were also catalytic to the development and growth of African nationalism and eventual African independence. It became quite evident to Africans that the doctrine and content of the missionary teachings were self-serving. Christian doctrine emphasised the idea that all human beings are made in the image of God and were Go's children equal in his eyes regardless of colour or nationality. Hence, it is endowed with the right to treat all humans with kindness and consideration. Nevertheless, not only did the church appear to never criticise colonial rule (which in all intents and purposes countermanded Christian teachings), but the missionaries themselves at times failed to put their doctrine into practice. They were disdainful of Africans and their rituals, customs and languages and, in some cases, deliberately attempted to destroy African institutions. They behaved as though they did not expect Africans to notice the contradiction between the benevolence of the doctrine and the virulence of the racism exhibited by some of the missionaries.

Africans were at times excluded from holding meaningful roles in the functioning of churches, and discrete social distance was maintained from Africans by interacting with them in a patronising manner and preaching the gospel not as a sacred calling but simply as a task to accomplish. Missionaries who had children, for instance, would send them abroad for education rather than to the same schools with African children and in colonies where European settlers had their own schools (for example in eastern, Central and southern Africa). The preference was to educate their children in racially exclusive schools, never questioning the morality of the existence of such segregated schools. By and large, except for scattered and isolated acts of defiance or opposition by a few missionaries to the forced labour or physical abuse of Africans, the churches wanted Africans to believe that colonisation was undertaken for the good of Africans.

While many Africans quietly endured, believing that obedience, humility and 'turning the other cheek' were necessary for their salvation, some others resented the inferior treatment and demanded to have a voice in running religious institutions. Some went on to establish their own churches where they could interpret the Scriptures in ways that allowed them to enjoy 'religious self-expression'. Examples include the Chilembwe church in Malawi, the Kimbangu and Kitawala churches in present DRC and the Tembu church in South Africa. However, the colonialists branded these churches 'cults'.

Additionally, education itself played a more catalytic role in developing African nationalism. Mission education was more or less inadequate with its emphasis on a religious education that even Western society was already finding anachronistic. But it was still able to whet the appetite of African people for more enlightenment and the awakening of their political consciousness, to question colonial authorities and to communicate their demands. It also turned out to be a powerful medium of African acculturation of Western Christian (and political) values as they were incorporated, to the utter surprise of colonial masters, into the political debate over the struggle for independence. Africans understood that education could equip them with more than just the ability to reading and writing, they wanted their children to acquire the intellectual skills and language abilities necessary to regain their land and to survive in the diaspora. A glimpse of this had been provided by colonial as well as missionary education.

Africans correctly believed that colonial authorities were more likely to deal with an educated African spokesperson than one who was not, and one who was also fluent in a relevant European language. Pioneer African leaders, including Jomo Kenyatta (Kenya), Léopold Sédar Senghor (Senegal), Julius Nyerere (Tanzania), Kenneth Kaunda (Zambia), Nnamdi Azikiwe (Nigeria), Hastings Kamuzu Banda (Malawi), were the products of missionary education in their countries. The 1950s and 1960s were especially important for the rise of nationalism and decolonisation, because the period, Europe's post-war golden age of economic growth, skill-intensive activities replacing labour-intensive ones, created the need for upgrading education.,

Besides equipping the African leaders, the church was sometimes also instrumental in political activism that demanded African freedom. For example, in South Africa, African pastors organised the first nationwide political movement to challenge a proposed racist legislation by the white minority government in 1912. In Kenya, African religious leaders opened up independent schools with political statements such as articulating the grievances of their people and allowing a mix of local and Christian beliefs. Unsurprisingly, the colonial government treated these schools as high-level security risks, further fuelling their motivation to demand independence.

WORLD WARS I AND II

World Wars 1 and 2 impacted African nationalism and the struggle for independence. Millions of Africans were drafted and served in both wars: one million in the First World War and two million in the Second World War. 700,000 Africans were enlisted by the British alone to fight on their side in World War II. The irony of using 'unfree' Africans to fight against the Nazis and to die for the freedom of the Allied countries was not lost on the African soldiers who saw military action in Europe, the Middle East and Africa itself.

The wars enabled African soldiers to learn modern military skills in battle with demonstrable leadership capabilities. They showed great valour in battle and earned the right to be respected. Their acts of bravery could have been deemed sufficient to banish any sense of inferiority and racist notions the West may have about Africans. However, after both wars, while their Western counterparts were rewarded with generous pensions and offers of lands in colonies, for their role in saving Britain and her empire, African soldiers were given handshakes and tickets for the journey back home. They could keep their khaki uniforms and nothing else.

These experiences of African soldiers weren't without consequence. Firstly, these African soldiers willingly used their new military and leadership skills to assist nationalist movements in fighting for freedom that were beginning to take shape in the colonies. Service in the colonial army had facilitated the meeting of Africans from different regions of the same colony, an important step in breaking down ethnic barriers and developing a shared identification with the country as a whole. Secondly, this interaction across ethnicities and the breakdown of ethnic barriers was greatly assisted by the common language gained from colonial education.

More importantly, however, there was the psychological impact fighting in the wars had on Africans: the dismantling of the myth of the white man's superiority. Due to the thorough and effective conquest of the African continent, a myth of the white man's superiority and invincibility had developed. This was nurtured through racial segregation policies in the colonies and harsh treatment of the 'natives'. He had behaved with impunity in Africa. The war experience significantly diluted this myth. African soldiers who had fought side by side with their white comrade in arms saw a range of emotions and abilities Africans knew they had too. It dawned on the Africans that beneath the skin, there was no difference between them and the Europeans.

According to the Zimbabwean nationalist, Ndabaningi Sithole, this eye-opening discovery had a revolutionising psychological impact on the African. It therefore became impossible to convince Africans that Europeans were some kind of superman. Discovering the successful exploits of Japanese soldiers, a presumably inferior, non-European people against the Russians in the Russo-Japanese War of the pre-World War I era and Japanese successes in World War II against the Allies—especially European colonial powers—contributed to breaking the myth as well.

To add to this, the wars were detrimental to the financial situation of European colonial powers. They were neither willing nor able to commit substantial resources to improve the dire social and economic conditions in the African colonies. And they had further depleted them by coercing Africans, who were even not able to produce enough to feed themselves, to produce primarily to feed Europe during the wars. This resulted in a considerable deterioration of agricultural conditions during and between the two world wars. Unemployment was high, rural–urban migration accelerated, resulting in overcrowded cities, and there were inadequate school and health facilities. The dire economic situation in Europe also made the European powers unwilling to militarily suppress the nationalist movements that had been fuelled by the devastation of the war. In fact, after the Second World War, a trend arose in Europe for an honourable exit from Africa, making the post-war economic situation in Europe not just a catalyst of African nationalism, but also a primary catalyst of African independence.

Europe's Golden Age of Economic Growth

Europe's successful economic recovery and exponential growth after the war provides a complementary perspective. It position Europe as economically capable of running its colonies but chose to direct its efforts to what it perceived were more urgent and more productive economic interests at home.

In the two decades of the 1950s and 1960s economic growth, not only in Europe but also globally, was exceptionally strong by historical standards. Even in Africa, many countries experienced robust growth at the end of the colonial period. These were in truth the boom years. in Europe, this period was marked by high rates of economic growth (especially in exports) without any serious interruption to economic activity, or financial and monetary crises, especially after the post-Second World War depression. Europe's economic strategy following the war on the one hand helped it to rebuild its infrastructure and industry and on the other, (even if unplanned) exploit production and supply alternatives to its colonial interests.

During this period of reconstruction, Europe's focus was on fostering economic cooperation across its continent and increasing its production output for export. International economic cooperation combined with investment in infrastructure and the ensuing output in production and priority placed on exportation led to increased outputs that outweighed demand, more efficient and less expensive supply chains through the unrestricted inter-Europe movement of people and goods and remarkable advancements in technology. These not only led to the economic boom, placing Europe in a very lucrative economic position but also arguably provided alternatives to the economic viability of managing its colonies.

France's Monnet plan is a good example of this. With its General Planning Commission established in 1946, France invested around $3 billion in six crucial sectors: coal mining, steel, electricity, rail transport, cement and farm machinery.

Europe's investment in production and infrastructure was accompanied by accelerated advancement in and application of, technological innovation. A high capital formation rate combined with the development of domestic market institutions, liberalisation of international trade and American (later Japanese) management methods and technology being applied in industry. On top of this, a large proportion of resources was devoted to research and development while education at all levels was invested in and continued to grow. The result of this was a high degree of technological innovation, especially in science-based industries such as chemicals, pharmaceuticals and electronics. The application of new inventions and rapid diffusion of techniques and technical developments in the major industrial countries also accelerated. Labour productivity was enhanced and cooperation between European states, which further increased the profitability of investments. In this way, technological advancements, beyond fostering efficiency, opened up alternative sources and methods of industrialisation and economic prosperity for Europe—more than its colonial operations.

Trade expansion through intra-European cooperation was a primary focus of its recovery efforts. Critical to this was to make the movement of people and products across European states easier through the removal of trade restrictions and reduction in tariffs and to create of a free trade area. This also facilitates the transmission of ideas, technological advancements and their spread, and the growth of trade. The high level of demand helped encourage the adoption of new products, especially in the field of consumer durable goods. This would eventually lead to the Organisation for European Economic Co-operation (OEEC) and cooperative agreements such as GATT (General Agreement on Tariffs and Trade) and the formation of trading communities like The European Economic Community (EEC) and The European Free Trade Association (EFTA).

The impact of this liberalisation policy is difficult to estimate precisely but there is no doubt that it resulted in the development of closer and more intricate cooperation among Western states and created greater trade opportunities among European countries further reducing interest in Africa. While Europe's golden age of economic growth may not have had a primary influence on African independence or any influence at all on African nationalism, the alternative prospects for economic prosperity it provided for the most part impacted the ease with which it withdrew from Africa.

It wasn't simply that post-war Europe lacked the financial wherewithal to adequately manage its colonies. It was also a deliberate redirection of its scarce resources towards rebuilding its own depleted economy and infrastructure. In any case, it can be said that the continent had recovered in time to hold on to its colonies without any adverse effect on its economy. Based on Europe's history with Africa at the time, its agreement to withdraw from Africa was uncharacteristically, mostly non-violent.

Europe had made the move from pre-colonial trade to imperialism when it was already benefiting from the African continent through trade and didn't necessarily need to colonise it. And the tools it used to advance its imperialism (its superior military, education, churches and most importantly, its African allies including local collaborators) were still readily available, even if depleted. Therefore, though other influences on African nationalism had an impact on Africa's struggle for freedom, the post-war economic fortunes of Europe played an important role.

Another nail in the coffin of colonialism was the League of Nations, set up after the First World War, with a directive that colonies under the control of Germany and Italy would be transferred as mandates to victorious Allied Powers. This was based on two conditions: the mandated territories had to be administered with a view to their ultimate independence and the European powers in charge of those mandated territories had to submit annual progress reports to the League on what they were doing to prepare the territories for eventual self-rule. Belgium, Britain, France and South Africa received such mandates. It was, therefore, only a matter of time before the idea of self-determination would extend to the other colonies as well. In practice, however, the League of Nations could not force the mandate powers to pursue progressive policies.

After World War II, the challenge of establishing a new world order that would prevent another mass-scale conflict was achieved when forty-six countries produced the founding charter of the United Nations Organization. The prior mandates system of the leagues was converted into the United Nations trusteeship system, overseen by a Trusteeship Council. Italy subsequently lost its entire African empire, as Eritrea was given to Ethiopia, which annexed it. Italian Somaliland became a U.N. Trust Territory and Libya was made a self-governing kingdom under the auspices of Great Britain. Both decisions, made without local input, would lead to trouble later.

Articles 62 and 73 of the United Nations Charter decried colonialism as unacceptable and that all European colonies in Africa and Asia had the fundamental right to govern themselves. The UN, therefore, became a forum for the leadership of the independence movements in African colonies to pressure their rights. Africa had the support of communist states like the Soviet Union, East Germany and Czechoslovakia, who were ideologically opposed to colonialism while countries like India willingly extended moral and material assistance to the African nationalist movements. The colonial powers were not receptive though and aimed to buy time. Portugal, for one, without any fear of disapprobation from her European allies, immediately moved to declare her African colonies as overseas provinces and, therefore, outside the purview of United Nations supervision.

The role of the United States in the post-World War II period is especially important for African decolonisation given that the United

States was not only a dominant global power but one which primarily wanted to expand its markets into the African continent and to get direct access to its rich resources. The post-1945 US support for the independence of African states was arguably part of the strategy for pushing Europeans out of the continent with the hope of establishing itself, in addition to other factors including geopolitical rivalry, ideological stance and domestic politics.

In this context, Pan-Africanism grew into a worldwide movement to encourage and strengthen bonds of solidarity between all ethnic people of African descent. As an ideology, it consists of two key elements: the common heritage of people of African descent and the common interests for their well-being. Three names have often been associated with Pan-Africanism—Henry Sylvester-Williams, W. E. B. DuBois and Marcus Garvey. While Sylvester-Williams has been credited with originating the idea of Pan-Africanism, Garvey and DuBois have been credited with propagating it.

Sylvester-Williams, alarmed by the frantic extension of colonial rule all over Africa and the racist treatment of Africans then living in London, summoned a meeting of Africans in 1900 to protest these actions to the British government and appeal to decent British people to do all they could to protect Africans from the depredations of the empire builders. The word 'Pan-Africanism' was born at that meeting to dramatise the need for them to work together to improve conditions facing them as people of colour. After Sylvester-Williams' death, the responsibility for continuing the work fell on an African-American intellectual and political/social activist, Dr DuBois.

DuBois felt that in order to free themselves from racial discrimination and racism, black people in the New World must reclaim their African roots and become proud of their heritage. Dubois' motivation was twofold. Firstly was the need to correct the history of Africans being severely mistreated for resisting colonial exploitation. Something had to be done to end the brutalisation of Africans by all colonial powers, ranging from forced labour, harsh punishment and concentration camps, and outright genocide.

Secondly, there was a need to seek recognition for the contributions made by African veterans in the First World War. Only European veterans were being rewarded for their efforts. Dubois' proposed that the Charter of Human Rights be amended for Africans as a reward for the sacrifices fighting for Allied Powers during the war. DuBois managed to gather support in the West. Petitions and resolutions at the conferences demanded that colonies be prepared for self-rule and that European powers shield Africans from abuse and set up a system to meet the legitimate demands of African people. The Pan-African conferences also demanded for education, the outlawing of forced labour and corporal punishment and political participation.

The biggest and, arguably, most impactful of these conferences was the one in 1945, attended by Africans from the continent, with African political parties, trade unions, youth leagues and students' associations sending representatives for the first time. The individual participants formed an impressive list of 'who's who of the black world' Many of them went on to lead their countries to independence, becoming prominent leaders that head high offices. This marked the transformation of the Pan-African movement from a protest movement in search of moderate labour, housing and healthcare reforms to a formidable force fighting for self-rule. The idea of independence was a dominant discourse at the conference. The conference permitted Africans in attendance to build credible relationships that later helped them organise their people when they returned home. The African activists in attendance were inspired by the resolutions and encouragement they received from one another.

Garvey's approach was quite different. Like DuBois, the premise of his struggle was that the lack of racial pride among black people was a key ingredient missing in the struggle for racial equality. He felt that the best way to redress the tribulations of black people was to return to Africa. His approach was to launch the Universal Negro Improvement Association (UNIA) in the hope that it would become a powerful movement but his more radical approach would eventually result in the deterioration of his relationship with the US black elite. Despite his personal and legal difficulties in the United States and his eventual eclipse, Garvey is credited with psychologically rehabilitating, after its vilification by the nineteenth-century racist ideology, the colour 'black', instilling an awareness in black people of their African roots and creating a real feeling of international solidarity among Africans and persons of African stock.

All in all, Pan-Africanism, a protest movement against racism has evolved into an instrument for anticolonial struggle dedicated to bringing about African rule in Africa. It inspired African leaders and intellectuals to hope that in the future, African states might be federated as the United States of Africa. Indeed, the efforts of African leaders like Dr

Kwame Nkrumah, who became the prime minister of the newly independent Ghana in 1957 were inspired by Pan-Africanism. It resulted in the convening of the sixth Pan-African conference in Accra in 1958. Nkrumah called it the All-Africa People's Conference. The conference attracted other and strongly opinionated leaders Patrice Lumumba of Congo and Tom Mboya of Kenya. That Africa will be free was not the focus but when and how soon. A few years later in 1963, the Organization of African Unity (OAU), a forum for all newly independent African nations was formed, with Nkrumah, Emperor Haile Selassie of Ethiopia and Gamal Abdel Nasser of Egypt playing pivotal roles. The contribution of Pan-Africanism to the successful development of African nationalism and the consciousness of people of African descent of connectedness to Africa is quite significant to Africa's struggle for independence.

It is also important to highlight the role of enlightened thinkers in Europe in the struggle for African independence. The system of colonial domination was antithetical to the basic Enlightenment principle that each individual is capable of reason and self-government as it involved a combination of slavery, quasi-feudal forced labour, or expropriation of property. Thus, Enlightenment thinkers such as Immanuel Kant, Adam Smith, Nicolas de Condorcet, Denis Diderot and John Stuart Mill, to name a few, argued against the legitimacy and dominant justifications for colonialism—the presumed responsibility to bring modernisation to the continent and the right to commerce which was understood to encompass not only trade but also missionary work and exploration. They were critical of the idea that Europeans had the obligation to 'civilise' the rest of the world. Diderot, for example, challenged the view that indigenous people were benefitting from European civilisation, arguing that European colonists were the uncivilised ones through their brutality, lack of restraint and instinct for violence.

In fact, it has been argued (more recently by the Nigerian philosopher Olufemi Taiwo) that Africa was on a path to modernisation before colonial occupation and the colonialists rather than enable it, obstructed, delayed and derailed it. Mill, recognising that a despotic government by a foreign people could lead to injustice and economic exploitation, identified a number of reasons why Europeans were not suited to governing colonies. Understanding local conditions were necessary for solving problems of public policies effectively which foreign politicians have very little of. Besides the cultural and religious differences meant there may be very little empathy in relations which results in tyranny. Where efforts were made to treat natives fairly, there was a high tendency of bias towards those similar to them such as colonists and merchants. Colonists and merchants go abroad in order to acquire wealth with little effort or risk, which meant that their economic activity was prone to exploiting the colonised country rather than developing it. These philosophers were key to critical movements within Europe that, together with Pan-Africanist movements, called out Europe for its imperialism and supported the self-governance of African states.

African Post-Colonial Independence

Winning political freedom from European colonial powers was but the beginning. Thriving as a non-subservient continent presents a very different challenge. The imbalanced relationship between the two continents continues, with Europe holding all the cards. This imbalance is serviced by a combination of factors that appear to keep the continent dependent on the West, in a relationship which, like in colonial times, remains beneficial to the West.

First and foremost, the sincerity of Europe's intentions regarding a free and independent Africa has always been doubted by many. Rather than objects of colonial subjugation, Africans seemed to have been transformed into partners in their own exploitation. This is illustrated by the now largely forgotten Eurafrica project. Conceived in the interwar years, the concept of Eurafrica evolved on many fronts in Europe, notably in parallel with the evolution of the Pan-European movement.

In the 1920s, when Richard von Coudenhove-Kalergi founded the first popular movement for a united Europe with his concept of a 'Pan European Union', he saw a Eurafrica alliance using the European colonial 'dowry' as an important factor for Europe to establish itself as a third pillar of global power in conjunction with those of the Americas and Asia. Many contend that these concepts played a key influencing role in the eventual structuring of the institutionalised relationships which finally emerged between independent African countries and the integrated Europe of the European Economic Community (EEC) and its successor, the European Union (EU).

Given this context, it is easy to draw the conclusion that the origins of the EEC and later the EU cannot be separated from the perceived necessity on the part of Europe to preserve, reform and reinvigorate the colonial system. It can be perceived as a plan to replace European colonial competition for Africa's resources with an internationalised colonialism that would allow Europeans to jointly exploit the continent under the auspices of the EEC (later EU), a mindset which would never really go away.

There were Africans who embraced the concept and didn't see it as degrading for Africa. The Senegalese author and first president of an independent Senegal, Léopold Senghor, favoured it as one which was connected both to his concept of négritude endorsing African cultural achievements and his vision of an African-European relationship in which both continents had parity in their levels of cultural achievements. But he probably did not see clearly the structural economic imbalances.

The expansion of the EU especially from the mid-1990s onwards has seen the core essence of the union shift away from the original founding members of the EEC and the colonial hubris they brought to a united Europe. The growth of the EU as an independent player in the international community has also dramatically increased the complexity of EU international relations away from the earlier situation.

Perceptions of the beginning of the institutionalised Africa-Europe relationship nevertheless remain largely tinted by aspects related to its colonial aspects. As such, similar to today's approach of the Chinese, following the First world war, Europe saw Africa as the place to get the resources needed to rebuild their broken economies to become a third superpower after the United States and the USSR. Africa's resources were often discussed in the creation of pan-European institutions. The Rome Treaty, in 1957 by the EEC, was an exact replica of the Berlin Conference's General Act 73 years earlier, which had sought to create an internationalised regime of free trade stretching across the middle of Africa.

In Rome in 1957, at the beginning of a formalised relationship between an integrated Europe and Africa, six European countries promised each other equal access to trading and investment opportunities in the territory of 21 African countries today, without the involvement of the Africans. Britain was not a part of the EEC treaty at first but it was soon obvious they had nursed similar ambitions for retaining control of their colonies. The British Chancellor of the Exchequer, Stafford Cripps famously said in 1947, that 'in Africa indeed is to be found a great potential for new strength and vigour in the western European economy'.

A decade later, in the same year, the EEC was set up, British Prime Minister Harold Macmillan commissioned a cabinet committee report on the effect of African independence on 'the prestige and influence of the UK' and whether 'premature withdrawal of United Kingdom jurisdiction would leave a vacuum which would be filled by a country hostile to the United Kingdom and her Allies'.

It was in this context that the countries of Africa were born as independent entities. Congenitally misshapen, they were easy prey for Europe. The Eurafrica project can be seen as having simply been given a makeover as the 1963 Yaoundé Convention signed between the EEC and 18 former French and Belgian colonies. Under the agreement, the Europeans allowed free access to their domestic markets to products from the African members, while the latter were, at least initially, permitted to impose restrictions on the entry of European goods into their territories in order to protect their own infant industries. Three years earlier, however, the UN Economic Commission for Africa had clearly warned that the arrangements would likely lead to economic dependency by tempting the Africans to prefer the short-run advantage of tariff concessions [in EEC markets] to the long-run gains of industrial development because the Europeans were unlikely to keep their markets open if the Africans actually decided to lock out EEC goods.

What the Portuguese attempted to maintain in Africa was in itself similar to some of the ways in which France attempted to incorporate Algeria into the French state. In the form of European overseas territories (OCTs) it is a continuing reality that there remain small territories in various parts of the world including Africa which are formally part of the European state. Unlike Brazil, which once was the location of the Portuguese monarchy, no African state hosted the rulers of a European country in the same way as Zanzibar was once the site for the ruler of the Arabian kingdom of Oman.

As regards an ongoing, strong European role in Africa, also of considerable relevance is the continuing existence of what is described as 'Françafrique', namely the French-speaking African countries which are a key focus for ongoing French political, economic and (especially) military interference in Africa. Following independence, France established a range of formal defence and military cooperation agreements with the French-speaking African states, later incorporating the former Belgian colonies of Burundi, Rwanda and Zaire within the agreements, all with the intention of protecting key, French economic interests (like uranium mines). One of the conditions for Niger's independence from France, for example, was a defence treaty that gave France priority access to its uranium which was deemed crucial to France's energy independence. Since then (until as recently as 2014), Niger received uranium royalties that are half the sums paid to Australia and Canada for their equivalent uranium reserves.

Arrangements like this gave France the authority to establish itself as a guarantor of hegemony and regional stability, by force, if necessary; a power that France, since then, has not hesitated to use. France's interventionist policy was centred around three pillars: First, a monetary pillar through the franc zone (14 African countries) sharing the same currency, the franc de la Communauté Financière Africaine (CFA), pegged to the French franc at a fixed parity. Second, the composition of a network of French experts present in the financial, institutional and educational structures as well as the state level of African countries. The third and perhaps most important the presence of French soldiers in several permanent bases scattered across the continent, as well as the presence of French advisers in African armies. Its military interventions ranged from preventing the escalation of violence to undercover military action to either ensure the survival of its African client regimes or to cause the collapse of others.

France's overt and covert military interventions affected Nigeria during the Biafra War), Senegal, Gabon, Chad, Mauritania, Zaire, CAR, Togo, Comores, Rwanda, Djibouti, Benin and Sierra Leone. In all but a few of these interventions, French action was to advance its economic interests, protect French nationals, subdue rebellion (irrespective of its legitimacy) and prop up pro-French rulers (and the suspected assassinations of anti-French rulers), including some of the most despotic and murderous individuals in post-colonial African history. It was seen in Paris as a way of remaining important and preventing American control over its resources.

Besides their debatable intentions, other colonial and post-colonial actions of Europeans laid the foundation that appears to keep Africa psychologically and subconsciously dependent on Europe. Carving up Africa across straight lines at the Berlin Conference in 1884 has had dire consequences, till today. This delusional process not only destroyed Africans' sense of belonging and patriotism, but it also laid the foundation for a crisis of trust and suspicion between citizens of the same country and people of different heritages). This drawing up colonial boundaries irrespective of age-old history, economy, culture, language, religion, etc. laid the foundation for a dualism between African states and African nations, one that tends to replicate many of the racially and ethnically prejudiced structures that were part of colonial rule. The result has been chaos and civil war (as old rivalries and enmities persisted) and further stagnation of growth and development and Africa's increased dependence on and interference by Europe (and the United States).

The demolition of pre-colonial government structures in Africa because of the scramble for Africa by the Europeans provides another example. What may have, on the surface, been the occupation of Africa by Europe was the destruction of pre-existing government structures. For Africans, it was symbolic of the collapse of a critical aspect of their political and cultural heritage, which provided guidance, stability and economic prosperity to their way of life. Its demolition and the imposition of somewhat contradictory systems has had not only a psychological impact but has also created tensions between both systems of government that in some way inhibit growth and, thus, Africa's continued dependence on Europe. The lasting transfer of different European governance systems (primarily by Belgium, France, Britain and Portugal) created additional fault lines in the continent.

On top of everything else, the actions of African leaders (across various levels—local to federal), has arguably been the most crucial factor that keeps the continent heavily reliant and subservient to the West. The rulers of post-colonial Africa have included some exceptionally corrupt and monstrous figures. They have plundered natural resources, syphoned public funds into their private enterprises, tortured and dehumanised their citizenry. They could never have done this, given their positions of influence, without the acquiescence of Europe supported by the United States.

Their actions have not only placed the continent at a disadvantage and, overly reliant on foreign assistance, they have also eroded the trust citizens are expected to have in their government. What is the point of investing in a new factory, if a ruler might suddenly throw you in prison for no good reason? What is the point of working hard for a degree, if the job will go to someone else? Why pay taxes if one knows they're simply going to pay for a birthday cake for a tyrant? Another consequence of this is the inferred permission for corruption given to other levels of government and society, which further places the continent at an economic and infrastructural disadvantage.

It is important to note, however, that the idea of corruption may be perceived differently in various African contexts. Many people who behave in perceived corrupt ways don't see it that way. They think they are doing the right thing; they believe they are being good. Due to Africa's Ubuntu and communitarianism roots, in many nations as soon as you come into a powerful job or get some money it is the custom to immediately dispense favours (contracts, positions/jobs, financial assistance) to your family. People will constantly grant these favours to members of their own group as opposed to those who might be most technically proficient or deserving. Referring to this as corruption (as defined in the West) overlooks its nuance.

In this way, the same Ubuntu that defines the social make-up of African interactions and relationships may also be a crucial factor in its continued subjugation to the West.

In decades since political independence, the relationship gradually expanded. Privileged access to the European market continued to be a key aspect of the relationship along with European development funding, both of which tended to continue echoes of colonial-style practices.

In April 2020, the ACP Group of States became an international organisation, the Organisation of African, Caribbean and Pacific States (OCAPS). It is this organisation which is currently responsible for finalising all aspects of the new agreement with the EU which was agreed upon and initialled in April 2021 (replacing the Cotonou Agreement formally expired on 29 February 2020). The fact that in late 2022 the OCAPS has been quoted in media as complaining that the Europeans are inexplicably delaying the next steps in the formal launch of the new relationship again tends to imply an unequal relationship in which Europe takes African goodwill for granted. The fact that separately the Economic Partnership Agreements (EPAs) between the EU and some ACP States or regional economic communities were designed, though many remain unfinished, adds to the unsatisfactory state of affairs. Many are those who believe that the EPAs have the collateral effect of in fact undermining Africa's own pathways to regional market integration, the EU and its member states pursue this course, nevertheless. Within the context of the institutionalised EU-African relationship, the question of whether Africa's position is truly free or independent remains therefore debatable.

The argument persists that in the EU-Africa interface African countries are simply being colonised differently, through destabilisation and manipulation to the profit of their former European colonisers. At the beginning of 1960 when African states gained their independence from the various European colonial and imperialist powers, they found themselves still entangled in a whole system of economic controls and conditions. Investor protection for example agreements limited the democratic space of African governments. These economic controls and conditions are an integral part of the various ways imperialists subjugate and transform peripheral states into neo-colonies. The strategies to maintain control include colonial debt, confiscation of national reserves and the right of first refusal on any raw or natural resource. But also military rights and access such as the right to train military officers, supply military equipment and the right to defend its interests by pre-deploying troops for military interventions in the country. Other strategies included the obligation to use colonial money (in West Africa), the obligation to make the colonial language the official language of the country and the language for education and money. Africa has not yet achieved the degree of full autonomy which former colonies in Asia have, often after more devastating interventions than all of Africa suffered (e.g. in South-East-Asia).,

Although the vast majority of African states achieved independence peacefully through negotiation, or all in all limited struggle compared to colonies elsewhere, it nevertheless makes a lot of sense to refer to the process of transition as a struggle. Africans were never simply asked: 'When do you wish to become independent?' They had to demand independence, they had to agitate for it. Many 'agitators' went to jail; some of them were banished from their own countries for long periods. It used to be said that the surest path to becoming prime minister of an English-speaking African country was through jail.

Many factors converged to mediate the struggle for independence: colonial education, the churches, ideas and expressions of support from individuals of African ancestry through the Pan-African movement, the exposure to the world through world wars and, of course, the forum provided briefly by the League of Nations and later by the United Nations. It is interesting that the Christian church and colonial education, pivotal tools in the Europeans' 'civilising missions' in Africa, also unintentionally became the tools that Africans would use in fighting for freedom. Despite the atomising impact of the divide-and-rule policies employed by colonial authorities, it is remarkable that Africans were able to create fairly unified movements. The key to this was the psychological shift that literary and practical education afforded Africans. And like it was during the struggle for colonial independence, education remains crucial to the struggle for post-colonial independence. The only other positive leftover from colonialism, at least in its later phase, are the public health systems.

CHAPTER 6

An Interdependency Stuck in the Past

African-European interdependencies go back to the beginning of time; they were more or less equitable, until the last two centuries. The sophisticated Egyptian Pharaonic kingdoms influenced via the Minoan culture on Crete ancient Greece. The first Greek trade settlement in Egypt dated from 7th BC. Egypt traded intensively with the ancient Kush (or Nubian) kingdoms, and they in turn traded with the kingdom of Great Zimbabwe and others down the Nile and further afield.

These relationships continued throughout the centuries, in Roman times and during the Arab and Ottoman dominance of the Mediterranean world, with different intensities. African states equally traded with the Arab and Indian world, and it is known that Chinese ships came to Eastern Africa, until the emperor decided in the fifteenth century to seal off China from the world.

Political order in Africa was no less organised, with rising and declining prosperity for the peoples, and overall its standards of living were like elsewhere in the known world. The great divergence would come only in the nineteenth century. Its economic, political and cultural development was different from Europe, Arabia, Persia or India, and yet the essence of its societies was comparable. The Kurukan Fuga (or Manden charter) in the Mali empire is a bill of human and civic rights, one of the first in the world (today a UNESCO intangible world heritage), dating from the same period as the English Magna Carta, and with the same purpose:

to give people the security to invest in learning, in food and artisanal production, and to trade.

The interactions moved with the vicissitudes of history, until the middle of the nineteenth century. In order to circumvent Venetian and Ottoman dominance of trade with India and beyond, Portuguese seafarers explored new routes around Africa. They founded trading posts, as did later the Dutch and others. Global economic developments, in particular the discovery and exploitation of the American continent and growing European trade across the Atlantic and with Asia, gradually weakened African economies. But until the end of the eighteenth century, trade relations dominated the interaction.

Then, in a short period of time, this changed as a consequence of the emerging industrialisation in Europe. Their ancient kingdoms, once admired, became easy victims for European armies, British and French, German and Belgian, and in the twentieth century also Italy sought to conquer its part of Africa. To justify these destructive incursions, a historically false narrative was developed. A contemporary comparison is the invasion of Ukraine by that other colonial power, Russia, which similarly extended its empire south and east, with a false narrative and brute military force, and also aimed at economic extraction and destruction of cultural identity. European military aggression, stoked by its mercantilism, destroyed the ancient political and social order in Africa and finally ruined its economies, leading to economic extraction and political dominance. The claim that Europe brought modernity to Africa has little evidence, on the contrary, colonialism may well have halted these countries' own evolution towards it. It also greatly increased inequalities inside these countries and between them and the colonising European countries, the consequences of which are felt today.

After the political independence of the newly crafted states, seldom corresponding to ancient ones, this false narrative has survived in many minds. It continues to hinder mutual cooperation and the emergence of a new fair and equitable relationship. The main player on the European side is now the European Union (EU), and several of its member states individually. It sought to deal with Africa on a two-track course, North Africa and sub-Saharan Africa, in addition to the pan-continental one that is slowly growing. They all follow colonial pathways, dressed up in new speak, barely hiding haughty Eurocentrism.

On the African side, the policy-making roles of African Union (AU), regional economic organisations and individual states is less clear, though the AU seems to emerge as the main political partner for the EU. They all fail to capture the new realities in Europe, to hold it to account for continuing economic extraction and social destruction, but they often fail to make themselves necessary systemic adjustments. However, in civic societies, new views are emerging, some based on evidence, others on woke waffle.

Asymmetric weaknesses plague the relationship and hinder fair and equal relations to the detriment of people on both continents. There are people of goodwill, here and there, but systemic weakness prevents significant results. In the post-colonial years, close cooperation has remained between Africa and Europe across many sectors making Europe (EU, with related countries) the largest foreign investor in Africa. Europe also remains the largest source of development aid for Africa, but this is not a blessing (except for its humanitarian aid in cases of emergency). For many years, the EU was the largest non-African trading partner with Africa but China reportedly overtook the EU in 2021 with bilateral trade between China and Africa rising 35% in that year alone to US$254 billion, and with exports from Africa into China totalling US$106 billion. Such diversification increases African country's strategic autonomy.

In 2022, emerging signs of new stability in North Africa after a decade of turbulence allowed further new cooperation between this region and the EU. These moves built on earlier European initiatives including the 1995 Euro-Mediterranean Partnership, also known as the Barcelona Process, which the EU intended to use to deal with, and coordinate, its relations with all the countries of the Mediterranean littoral. In 2008, the Partnership was subsumed into a newly established Union for the Mediterranean which aimed to promote stability and integration throughout the Mediterranean region among other things by bridging the European-North African regions. The jury is still out on whether it has any meaningful impact.

The relationship between Europe and Sub-Saharan Africa has been more focussed and remains of special pivotal relevance to the broader Africa-Europe interface. In this, the EU-ACP relationship remains of central relevance, but it is a relationship that is part of the problem and that needs fundamental adjustment to the current times. The entire setup between the ACP states and the EU is still more rooted in the colonial past than in a strategic view of the future, not least because some EU member states prefer it that way. Such perception is further heightened by the fact that in the ACP-European relationship, the Europeans, not yet cured of condescendence, are seen to be holding a position of economic as well as political power over the African countries.

Though on 1 January 2021, the African Common Free Trade Area was formally launched, its Agenda 2063, of which it is part, is more than a generation away, long enough for African politicians to avoid tackling the vested interests which hinder its realisation. In fact, the same African leaders continue to support the ACP Agreement with the EU, duplicating efforts, undermining a coherent strategy and maintaining an in essence neo-colonial framework, which apparently suits and benefits those in power. The European Commission and African, Caribbean and Pacific countries, known as the ACP Group, initialled a renewed Cotonou Agreement, which at the time of writing still is blocked by one EU member state (Hungary), which the others could circumvent if they really wanted. Never mind, it would bring no game change anyway, path dependency is more convenient than creative adaptation to new contextual conditions.

The Original Sin

It is impossible to really innovate the African-European relationship to mutual benefit given their multidimensional interdependence, without going back to the roots of the distortions, that is to the beginning of the eighteenth century. Industrialisation in Europe and colonialism go hand in hand.

Modern economic research has shown convincingly that European industrialisation was based on extensive extraction of raw materials and energy from the rest of world, and that this was done not on fair trading terms, but on unequal ones supported by military invasions, destruction of the institutions and culture of these ancient countries, commoditising slavery, deliberately ruining competitive economic sectors through protectionist policies, and subjugation of people in colonial empires which institutionalised racism and inequality in African societies till the times of political independence. In the later decades, African health and education provisions were replaced by European models, designed for the new economic needs, but their benefits still pale in comparison to the structural inequality in the colonial relationship.

There are specific political and cultural reasons why Europe could economically advance in that period of time over the rest of the world, whereas before economic developments had been more or less comparable in the world and national wealth had not been greatly divergent. Key among them are the advances made in food production, made possible by new techniques and massive deforestation, by strengthened central state administrations and taxation systems, and by expansion of its military. Enlightenment philosophy played an important role in opening the minds and making scientific rationalism the key tool for organisation of the market economy; democratic government, including extension of human rights, facilitated its social penetration and consumption-based economic growth.

No doubt this historic period brought humanity more advances than any other before, in education, public health and overall living conditions, but it was limited to Europe, later North America and later Japan. However, globally it led to greater inequality and to more ecological destruction than ever before. European welfare state systems developed in the late nineteenth century dealt with the first and brought more social equality internally. But on a global scale, the new levels of inequality persist and the ecological consequences are only now slowly being treated.

Neo-colonial attitudes in Europe today are rooted not only in a hidden continuation of colonial thinking and in vested interests but they have become mixed up with Eurocentrism, a loot of Occidentalism, a world view about Western supremacy, born during this period of philosophical Enlightenment, economic industrialisation and political and military expansion. Occidentalism ignores the major contributions of other world regions to humankind's development. It is important to realise the role of this subconscious mental framework that distorts even good intentions.

Occidentalism leads to unease and ambiguity, even hate, which people all over the world feel for the basic tenets of so-called Western modernism and what it has done and still does to their ancient societies. It is their response to the condescendence of Westerners so well described by Edward Said and many anticolonial thinkers (including enlightened Westerners), and to the destructions Europeans inflicted on the world for centuries, beginning with the conquest and destruction of the American indigenous civilisations, later followed by the subjugation of others during the times of colonialism. It has long been plastered over in Western minds with distorted historic teaching and one-sided media reporting, but not in theirs. The internal struggles all over the world to incorporate the material benefits of Western modernity with the preservation of the soul of their ancient societies and culture are still ongoing. History in the globalised world today is not synchronic, next to rapidly modernising countries, there are others that cling to past ways of living or are trapped in neo- and post-colonial conditions. All want to preserve some social and cultural identity in the face of particularly crude American materialism and its missionary zeal to spread its capitalist version of a market economy. Europe could be a moderating force in this world in transition, but it has started to follow the same path since the 1980s, weakening its more socially corrected market economies, with their post-war welfare distribution mechanisms, pushing trade agreements abroad but ignoring local collateral effects. Its slightly asymmetric market opening with some economically weak countries is a political gesture with negligible systemic effect on economic transformation in these countries.

This current Western but mainly American economic model has become a travesty of the original Enlightenment philosophy on which it claims to be based. These ideas were not only the basis of the scientific-rationalist development which led to industrialisation and modernity, but they also strongly defended humanistic and moral values. Enlightenment philosophers, such as Adam Smith or Nicolas de Condorcet, placed high emphasis on them; the latter was the first to claim the abolition of slavery (in the French colonies).

In the last decades, these Enlightenment values have been neglected too often, with ecological destruction and rising inequality as a consequence; it may ultimately even erode democracy itself, as political events in some countries indicate. The Indian Foreign Minister Subramanyam Jaishankar openly speaks of the West's hypocrisy. This is nowhere clearer than in Europe's refugee and migration policy. Western governments still believe that they can impose market regulations, often well-intended, or monetary dominance, without prior consultation and consent and without taking into account the impact on other countries.

The establishment of global institutions after the Second World War, when colonialism was still very much in existence, did not help. Today, they date from a world that is disappearing. When contextual conditions change, institutions must adapt to remain relevant and efficacious. But this will be resisted by the beneficiaries of the original arrangements, understandable but short-sighted, while the newcomers may not have yet the levers for change. African countries find themselves in such a position.

This Occidentalism has the ingrained habit since the nineteenth century of interpreting the world exclusively through the narrow spectrum of modernism and short-term material interests, leading to a technocratic approach that excludes many intangible elements important for other peoples. Statistics do not offer inclusive analysis. This has been side-lined in Western parlance, but people all over the world do not think in the Western ways. Political leaders are predominantly framed by their national systems, and they have yet to realise the consequences of this myopic approach in the new geopolitical context.

Eurocentrism is the variant of this ideology that sees the whole world, even neighbouring countries which could be understood more easily and better, through the keyhole of EU institutional interests. Europe has a grand model of integration and exemplary welfare state models, and the rest of the world should follow it. European integration mechanisms certainly provide a unique model for countries to jointly manage common interests, be they economic or ecological. But Eurocentrism dispenses to spend time and effort on understanding the complexity and interdependencies of today's globalised world. It lacks self-criticism and leads to an exclusive technocratic approach, ignoring the importance of soft but equally real issues, such as history, religion and culture.

As a consequence, Europe still lacks strategic empathy, which facilitates the hidden survival of colonial views. The French political analyst Dominique Moisi has shown in a remarkable book in 2009 the importance of emotion in geopolitics. Hope, fear and humiliation are important drivers. Historical grievances from Europe's colonialism and America's multiple wars, the awareness, thanks to new media, of their own poverty compared to the West's wealth and waste of resources, the West's hypocrisy in supporting authoritarian and exploitative regimes wherever it suits them, it all contributes to tensions which require different mindsets, in the mutual long term interest. But it often conflicts with its short-term economic interests, and they mostly dominate the actions behind the talk. Democratic systems have problems with foresight and strategy, leadership and change management.

After the Second World War, Europe tried to develop a new narrative to do away with extreme nationalism. Nothing of the sort was attempted after the end of colonialism. On the contrary, the nineteenth-century European fallacy that it had to 'civilise' Africa has been simply updated for the twentieth-century post-independence reality that it has now to 'develop' Africa. The Schuman Declaration, and European policies ever since, prove that they are conceptual twins.

The Long Twilight of Colonialism

It is often said that it takes three generations for an event to become history, i.e. no longer part of living memory. It can, of course, linger on in the collective consciousness for much longer, as a tranquil memory, or be stirred up artificially by contemporary political interests. Therefore, the geopolitical context in the 1950s, which inevitably influenced the Founding Fathers of the European integration process, cannot be overlooked. Its background determined Europe's relationship with Africa immediately after independence, and it caused the path dependency of Europe's policy design towards Africa which has hindered a game change ever since.

In 1954, France lost the battle of Dien Bien Phu and had to withdraw from Indochina. In the same year, the war of independence in Algeria started. In 1956 the Suez crisis, caused by France and Britain, made it clear that colonial-style expeditions were over. Belgium still ruled the Congo, impervious to the signs of change in Africa, where independence movements had sprung up everywhere. France and Britain were trying to suppress them with brutal repression and military interventions; Portugal would do the same, and Belgium just walked away. The trauma of losing Indonesia in 1949, after a four-year war, was still fresh in Dutch minds. Britain actively supported the harsh and humanly degrading South-African apartheid regime, of which it had led itself the basis.

The Schuman Declaration (1950) was doubtless a visionary, new departure for Western Europe. It led to the establishment of the European Coal and Steel Community (ECSC, 1952), followed by the European Economic Community (EEC, 1957), the direct precursor of the European Union (EU). It was the beginning of structural transformations which led to the basis of its current economic strengths and people's welfare.

It was far less a new departure for Africa. In the original text, colonial views prevalent at the time were clearly present. The Schuman Declaration said 'Extra means will become available to allow Europe to fulfil one of its most essential tasks, the development of Africa'. The sentence was later taken out to fit Europe's self-image as a bringer of peace and prosperity but re-instated after the publication of Swedish research in 2014.

Economic interests played a key role. Germany had no access to minerals in Africa since 1918. The French and Belgian governments wanted to entice it and assumed that it would be in the common interest of the original six signatories to keep Africa as a market for agricultural and industrial products. African trade had been mutually beneficial for centuries, though global trade patterns became a source of Africa's economic decline in the sixteenth to eighteenth centuries. In the 1950s, the relationship was even seen as a way to help solve Europe's unemployment problem by stimulating migration to Africa. There was talk during the negotiations of an association, later of a free trade area, with the colonies.

Consequently, the Treaty of Rome (1957), setting up the EEC, included African countries in a sort of neo-colonial European-African vision, based on bringing 'development'; while 'civilising' was the nineteenth century justification for Europe's colonialism, the 'developing' is its new version of the twentieth century. Leaders of Africa's independence movements and of newly independent states did not want to hear about it. Many countries became independent in the year 1960. Algeria followed in 1962. Little was left of Europe's imperial visions.

In order to hastily protect its vested interests, in 1963 the EEC signed the Yaoundé Treaty with the Association of African States (18 in total), which was renewed in 1969 and 1971. In 1975 it was replaced by the Lomé Convention, later renewed by the Cotonou Partnership Agreement. The number of countries increased in step with their independence, and former Caribbean and Pacific colonies were added. The fact of heaping together countries so different is another indication of the basically colonial and technocratic mindset. Today, there are 79, on three continents, with very different political, economic, social and cultural backgrounds or prospects. Behind grandiloquent declarations, the main purpose was invariably to maintain economic dependence and political leverage, compensated with development aid, distributed mostly according to European objectives.

For many years, two key elements of this EU relationship with the ACP countries have been privileged trade access to the European market on a non-reciprocal basis in favour of the ACP states and soft 'development' finance from the European side. In practice, this maintained colonial trade patterns and contributed little to the structural transformation of African economies. It was not alien either to authoritarianism and corruption in African countries. It also tended to entrench the attitude of many Europeans dealing with the ACP from a superior position and not one between equals. A new agreement with the EU, which was agreed and initialled by both sets of negotiators in April 2021, has not yet been implemented because the Europeans have failed to formally approve it (due to opposition of just a couple of member states with no interest for Africa). The new agreement though contains some major changes which implicitly recognise that the current situation cannot go on indefinitely.

The delay in the new ACP (or OACPS)-European agreement inhibits reform and progress on the broader EU relationship with Africa and maintains the status quo. European moves to expand the political aspects of the relationship rather than have it solely focussed on development are met with suspicion. Ironically, although this should be appealing to the Africans in so far as it should mean according to them more status than only being the recipients of economic support, the manner in which the Europeans have been handling the process still reeks of Eurocentrism leading to continued African dissatisfaction. Moreover, it ignores the important role of civic society and of enterprises.

Changes in the ACP-EU relationship, especially those that seemingly undermine what were assured economic benefits for Africa, together with European attempts to get African endorsement of European preferences on political matters, could now allow the Europeans to be increasingly perceived as using a political agenda to hold Africa hostage economically, and this could further damage African perceptions of Europe and enthusiasm for the partnership. In the medium to long term though, a more assertive Africa will help a new generation of Europeans to leave behind attitudes rooted in the colonial past.

One of the key, new features for the ACP states in the new agreement has been increased, regional structuring of the group along their three, basic geographic regions (i.e. Africa, the Caribbean and the Pacific). Three regional protocols for the three groups set out detailed sets of strategic priorities, often with additional notes referring to specific regional frameworks (for example regarding AU programmes in the case of Africa). Belatedly, the agreement also regionalises the joint ACP-EU institutions, including regional summits, councils of ministers, regional joint (ambassadorial) committees and parliamentary assemblies.

This represents a major shift towards the regional protocols for the ACP parties in their relationship with the EU, yet simultaneously the new architecture retains all the existing joint institutions (the OACPS-EU council of ministers, the OACPS-EU ambassadorial committee and the joint OACPS-EU parliamentary group). This has further increased the complex clumsiness of the ACP–EU relationship and reduces its flexibility and impact in the real economic world. Instead of improved coherence investors and traders get more complexities, duplication and uncertainties.

But the issue of privileged access to the EU by the ACP countries was already hit by a radical change introduced by the Cotonou Agreement of 2000 when the non-reciprocal trade preferences previously granted to the ACP countries were to be replaced by the envisaged system of Economic Partnership Agreements (EPAs) between the EU and regions of the ACP countries. The EPAs provided for reciprocal trade agreements that conformed to World Trade Organization (WTO) requirements. This allowed for ACP exports to get duty-free access to the EU on condition that ACP countries also provide duty-free access to their own markets for EU exports. Not all ACP countries needed to comply, those belonging to the category of Least Developed Countries (LDCs) were able to continue under the trade terms of the Lomé Convention or the liberal 'Everything But Arms' (EBA) regulations. Non-LDCs that didn't feel able to enter into EPAs could be transferred to the EU's Generalized System of Preferences (GSP) or the Incentive Arrangement for Sustainable Development and Good Governance (GSP +).

The flexibilities regarding trade allowed for in the Cotonou Agreement did not stop the Africans criticising the EU for treating them unfairly, and to continue to try to 'divide and rule' in classic colonial style. It was seen as an attempt to undermine new African moves towards a pan-African free trade area. Many African countries also claimed that the EPAs would undermine their local industries in a variety of ways.

In fact, recent years show a struggle between new and old ideas, forward-looking policy proposals and firmly vested interests, and this has led to small incremental changes, instead of innovating fundamentally the whole relationship and cutting it free from its colonial roots. Meanwhile, imperial dreams had not disappeared either. In 2007, French President Sarkozy launched the idea of 'EurAfrique' and other European leaders would echo similar ideas, driven by internal political concerns and economic interests. It led at the 2nd Africa-Europe Summit in Lisbon in the same year to the launch of Joint Africa-Europe Strategy (JAES). The concept of an AU-EU Partnership remained part of the political mantra in the EU institutions, but less so in Africa. It came back at the African-European Summit in Abidjan (2017) but the focus was put now on youth when European leaders started to realise that millions of jobs would be needed in Africa if not unmanageable migration streams would continue. Commission President Juncker reiterated the idea in his annual State of the Union speech to the European Parliament in 2018 with the call for an Africa-Europe Alliance for Investments and Jobs. In March 2020 this was followed by a new EU comprehensive strategy with Africa and another Summit in February 2022 where fine diplomatic speaking masked the absence of substance and a concrete roadmap for implementation once again. Facts and figures point to a massive lack of impact of 15 years of political exorcism. Parallel to the EU relationships with Africa within the OACPS context and the various arrangements with North Africa, the new European strategy to engage Africa at the continental level is however a new reality of the Africa-Europe interface, but at the moment it adds only to legalistic complexity.

It remained within a traditional technocratic and Europe-centred approach, lacking substantial innovation in line with new contextual conditions. There is no recognition that Africa's problems are rooted in Europe's colonialism and no strategy to assist African countries to amend this. Many economists recognise that its economic woes are linked to neo-colonial economic relations. However, there is no talk of intelligent, future-oriented reparation. European leaders like to talk, among themselves, about African countries' poor governance. They have a point, but they forget the main cause. The colonial state organisation was alien to the pre-existing states, it was a regime of military occupation. After independence, African leaders had no means to fundamentally reconnect the state and society. Incompetent and corrupt dictators could grab power because of the weakness of state institutions alien to the people, not seldom with the military help of European governments. A new generation starts to see this dichotomy and to act on it, but it will be a difficult and long process of reform.

Path dependency in EU policy goes back to a classic problem in international organisations, whose members are sovereign states, which have pooled parts of their sovereignty. Today technological innovations or geopolitical developments can rapidly make existing policy, and the regulations, procedures and funding accompanying it, less efficacious or even obsolete, either in its prescription and/or in its application. This results not only from the fact that changing contextual conditions would require change, even a game change but also because it leads to adaptation by the addressees. But one policy is often followed by others, based on the same concepts which meanwhile may have become bypassed or even counter-productive.

Once such a policy trajectory is opened up, new (public and private) interests grow upon it which prevent timely or substantial innovation, including simply pausing or definitively halting. The rigidity of purpose is often linked to a public good, but it should not necessarily be accompanied by rigidity of methods, in particular not when dealing with complex issues. Just continuing a particular trajectory without regular checks of its impact and costs, and without re-examination of the objectives themselves, is the main cause of excessive regulatory burden and costs. In the end, there is little or no benefit left, and citizens increasingly consider the system illegitimate. Strategic agility, now generally accepted in business, is difficult to realise in these political-bureaucratic systems, relying heavily on legalistic procedure and complicated decision-making processes, often hindered also by internal political developments in (influential) member states.

Thus over the years, a number of other policy frameworks and instruments were heaped upon Africa by the EU, such as the Joint Africa-Europe Strategy, the European Economic Partnership Agreements (EPAs) and more, often well-intentioned, but all adding to policy incoherence, asymmetries and political and bureaucratic competition inside the European Commission and between it and the newer EEAS (European External Action Service). A European Development Fund (EDF) channelled billions of Euros in aid, but its contributions to African structural economic adjustments are minimal. It does not even compensate for the average EU's annual trade surplus. Some development aid had a positive micro-economic impact or helped to alleviate the worst kind of poverty and humanitarian crisis, but it did not lead to structural transformations. The 'White Saviour Industrial Complex', as a Nigerian intellectual coined it, continues to haunt Africa. Africans are rightly sceptical, given a variety of examples that seemingly deny EU claims of sincerity about the bi-continental partnership.

In September 2018, the then EU Commission President Jean-Claude Juncker stressed that the new EU-African relationship should move beyond a donor-recipient approach to an 'alliance of equals'. In March 2020, the new President of the EU Commission, Ursula von der Leyen, and the new High Representative for Foreign Affairs and Security Policy, Josep Borrell Fontelles, proposed a basis for a 'Towards a Comprehensive Strategy with Africa' which proposed intensified cooperation in five key areas, namely green transition, digital transformation, sustainable growth and jobs, peace and governance and migration and mobility. These were accompanied by ten related 'actions' which were largely economic and included facilitating investment in Africa and its business climate.

The reality of the Europeans habitually confronting the Africans with a pre-written programme that often especially suits EU priorities, without many prior consultations, continues to be a problem. Grand statements for the media and home electorates are misleading, in practice European funding is primarily available for projects which respond to European priorities.

The 6th AU-EU Summit, postponed due to the coronavirus pandemic, was finally being held in February 2022 in Brussels. It closed with a joint declaration 'A Joint Vision for 2030' and an EU pledge for 150 billion euros for the period 2021–2027 which was delivered through the 'Global Gateway' scheme of 'Team Europe' (EU and Member States), a new effort at better coordination and coherence between EU and member states activities in Africa. If implemented in a true partnership spirit, then it could be a more significant improvement than anything before. The joint declaration of the 'renewed Partnership' states that the partnership addresses immediate and long-term opportunities as well as challenges, such as joint action to promote peace and security, address migration and mobility issues, support Africa's green energy transition to climate neutrality, and to promote multilateralism in addressing a range of issues including those relating to health and global public goods.

Whatever economic progress Africa made was primarily thanks to new technologies (ICT in particular), the global price rise of minerals, some IMF-induced reforms (after its ill-considered earlier interventions), local market increases due to rapid population growth, to name but a few. And not forgetting Chinese investments. There were private sector investments from Europe and equally a few African multinationals invested in Europe. It is not really an overstatement to say that many member states of the AU, with few exceptions (such as Egypt), for the most part experienced what would later be true of South Africa after the end of apartheid: political freedom without economic empowerment.

Independence movements that took over colonial government structures were caught between the West, bent on maintaining economic dependence, and the Communist bloc aiming to export its system. Governance reform was not a priority nor a realistic option. Interventions by the UN and IMF, Africa's own slow awaking of a post-colonial consciousness, American and European policies all combined to prevent Africa from doing what the south-east Asian tigers were able to do. There are many reasons why the structural transformation of the African economies still has to take off. Without that however, there will be no chance of creating jobs for the millions of young people coming onto the market every year and emigration will remain their only rescue. There will be no partnership of equals with Europe either.

The mental frame for European colonisation in the nineteenth century was comparable everywhere in the world. The ancient grandeur and serenity of Africa, which appears so clearly from earlier travellers' reports, was forgotten. Its great influence on the development of modern art in Europe and on music in the Americas was not enough to penetrate and change the overall narrative. Africa has no history, Europeans thought, ignoring ample historic evidence, because they needed a justification for their colonial empires and economic exploitation. Africa's economic development before the scramble for Africa in the nineteenth century was not significantly deviating from elsewhere in the world and it could have evolved further, but for the colonial dismembering of its economic structures. The old aristocratic and business elites in African kingdoms which resisted colonisation were annihilated, repression was merciless everywhere.

Today, ignorance mixed with remnants of the colonial past linger unconsciously in the minds of many Europeans, sometimes even more in those without colonies. There is still high-mindedness in European governance circles, in media and in business, about how other countries should copy the European model; other large powers equally try to control in many ways their near neighbourhood. The millennial history, ancient cultures, and social structures of these countries are relegated to travel guides, they are hardly used as input for new policy, alongside contemporary evidence. Till recently, Africans have too easily submitted to these attitudes, or they have cleverly used it to prevent objective criticism of their own policy errors.

Reparation of the Minds

Europe's own history and diversity could better prepare it to understand Africa's than any of its geopolitical competitors if it would dare to look colonialism straight in the eye and draw the inevitable consequences. If they were to follow its own precepts in practice, Europe (in case of the EU) could become a preferred partner for other countries. But it has given itself over to governance by accountancy and statistics, side-lining historic, cultural or social understanding, ignoring the deeper currents which run through societies. Churches and courts have been the source of great cultural developments, technocracies are culture indifferent. How can one expect then empathy for people with different aspirations?

History provides useful lessons for a real, equitable, future partnership. How many Europeans involved in Africa are knowledgeable about the writings of African philosophers such as Kwame Apiah, Achille Mbembe or Leopold Senghor, to name but a few? How many are even aware of the studies by European scientists such as Leo Frobenius or Leo Apostel who tried to penetrate the essence of the ancient and rich African philosophical and social thoughts? It could help to understand their counterparts and it would surely lead to humility and respect simultaneously, besides being instructive for Europe itself. How many European officials dealing with Africa know its pre-colonial history? European school manuals still focus on Europe's historical links with Africa, not on Africa's own history. How many have indulged in its great literature, a source for deeper understanding, during the long flights to Africa, instead of only looking at figures and statistics? How many speak an African language (Swahili, Yoruba, Omoro, Hausa, Zulu and others, all spoken by tens of millions of people)? How many experts from the African diaspora work in EU institutions, or in national ministries? How many know the Manden Charter, a bill of rights of the Mali Empire? The gaps in the EU Commission library about Africa are revealing.

Forging a Constructive Interdependence

Europe after the Second World War has had a number of constructive experiences with reconciliation processes, such as the Franco-German Reconciliation Treaty. It is illustrative of the narrowing of minds that no such efforts were made after the collapse of colonialism or communism. These initiatives have led to a number of specific actions to positively influence the minds of people and thus create a new social-cultural paradigm. This has facilitated the work of politicians to steer the necessary process of economic integration and political cooperation. The EU has at times included some minor activities which could contribute to launching such a broad, new narrative, but they were isolated and without a coherent strategy. However, it shows that the need to do something was already recognised. A new departure is needed now and it is possible, that Europe focusses its thinking on African realities instead of European perceptions and on African initiatives instead of European wishful thinking. There should be a new, common, agreed narrative as a priority for future collaboration. Thinking grand, and symbolic gestures are missing.

The asymmetries between both political systems are a real hindrance, as much as the conceptual weaknesses and the undigested histories. Resulting from different historic origins and operating in different contextual conditions, the objectives, the division of powers, the administrative capacities and the decision-making procedures between African and European institutions are not aligned.

African states are the successors of the artificially divided ancient kingdoms and the economic extraction systems of European colonisers. They have not grown organically and many are still in the process of constructing sovereign nation-states on the Westphalian model whereas economic globalisation and ecological challenges require nowadays less sovereignty and more cooperation and integration between states. The small elites which achieved independence have more or less taken over these colonial states and their economic structures, but there is another Africa that lives on, based on the pre-colonial social and economic realities. The gaps and links between the two are complex and often misunderstood.

Technology and trade are drivers of interdependence which has consequences for the contemporary role of states. They stimulate the creation of prosperity but they also limit national decision-making space. The external constraints on internal policy-making differ according to individual states' contextual conditions, such as natural economic resources or research and innovation capacities. But every state in today's globalised world experiences external impacts on internal policies; they try to deal with this in two ways, by exercising counter-pressure, a preserve of a few very large powerful states, or by cooperating and integrating. The gradual reform of the African Union and the creation of Agenda 2063 and in particular the launch of the AfCFTA indicate that this process is now on its way; it will facilitate Africa becoming the master of its own economic, ecological and social paths to future prosperity.

The AU process of policy-making is not structured as in the EU, its institutions have not yet crossed the crucial legal line between supranational and international. Probably they should not even try to emulate the EU model, which emerged in contextual conditions fundamentally different from the current ones in Africa. But it surely cannot avoid overcoming the downsides of the Westphalian state model imposed on Africa during colonialism and designing itself an original pathway towards state cooperation and economic integration, involving its civic societies and business communities.

Its economies are not yet intertwined as the EU ones have become since the launch of their Common, later Single Market processes, in respectively 1957 and 1985. In 2021, intra-African trade stood at barely 15% of countries' trade, whereas in the EU it is far over 50% for all member states (except Ireland, because of the post-Brexit trade with the UK). This is not, as Europeans like to think, a consequence of incompetence, but of economic structures imposed by them, still partly and covertly controlled by them, including corruption and military interventions. Individual African states have fewer incentives to cooperate, but in a world driven by new technologies and globalised value chains, which facilitates the growth and innovation of small and medium-sized enterprises, that is one of the causes of slow economic adjustment. However, there are also examples of global corporations which operate successfully and fairly in Africa.

An EU-Africa strategy cannot be efficient if it does not find some way to take into account the 54 AU countries and their still larger, structural, economic diversity than what exists between the EU 27 after many decades of economic integration. But strategising and managing foreign relations are precisely a weak point of the EU, except in trade. Operational flexibility is difficult to achieve in rigid, treaty-based organisations of (semi-) sovereign states, even more so if a coherent and inclusive vision is lacking and short-term calculations and vested interests, including those of the 'white aid industrial complex', dominate.

The EU is basically an experimental system of governance, with a mixture of federal and inter-governmental characteristics, and forever evolving. This creates a problem for African states dealing with the EU. With limited government capacities, also for managing their global interests, they are confronted with an original and complex policy-making system, which requires permanent and careful monitoring, coordination and flexibility, and coherent operations with the EU institutions (Commission and Parliament) and the 27 individual member states simultaneously. The EU is confronted with the fault lines between new African states and their traditional societies. This makes it difficult to build lasting connectivity and limits its dealings with those in power. There are no systemic research efforts to better understand each other's political economy, the roots of successes and failures found in history and sociology. Technocratic systems are impervious to analysis which cannot be captured in facts and figures, they do not consistently include historic and social analysis, and thus they consistently miss an important part of understanding societies. There are of course enlightened individuals in such systems, but the levers for change are many and need to be operated in unison. Otherwise, stagnation continues, effectiveness declines, and so does legitimacy, because technocratic systems, more even than classic democratic governance, need delivery to maintain citizens' support.

In addition, the EU policy-making mechanisms, intended to establish a common market, later a single market and a monetary and economic union, have not been fundamentally adapted to the needs of new policies either. The EU struggles whenever it sets itself new strategic objectives. In fact, this is true for Africa as well, both continents are confronted with a classic system steering problem. Instead of seeking to fit new policies into existing steering models designed for other objectives, the operational models need to be adapted to the new policies, as systems theory explains. When one is faced with paradigm shifts, when too many anomalies and dysfunctions occur simultaneously in a particular context and when these can no longer be explained within existing thinking frameworks, innovation of the system governance is required, involving a radical shift of mindset and of operational modes.

A move towards the priority of efficacy of delivery, instead of process, complementing political-legalistic thinking about competences with modern management methods, with a focus on innovation replacing path dependency, and better adjusted to a digital age, would give the EU and the AU, new vigour, credibility and legitimacy. Now one is faced with two organisations of member states which are both struggling to adapt their organisation and operations to future needs and current contextual conditions, and with precarious credibility with citizens.

Given the steering role of the Heads of Government in the EU, a recent development in the EU, can perhaps be helpful. In the last decade, there has been a power shift from the EU Commission to the European Council, because democratic legitimacy of heads of state and governments appeared essential to achieve solutions in crisis situations or to agree on strategic directions in new policy sectors. This is a form of Europeanisation of national policy-making. But it would still require operational modernisation inside the EU institutions and appropriate operational convergence and capabilities in the member states. Today, there is a capacity problem, at least in parts of the EU institutions, and there are more obstacles than incentives for common policy-making; as a result, delivery is below expectations.

In the AU, a strengthening of the capabilities of the common institutions is an equally urgent task, though the many autocrats among its heads of government are less likely to accept a proper system of checks and balances than nearly all liberal-democratic government leaders in Europe. Nevertheless, ancient African forms of governance and consensus building, aided by digitalisation, could inspire innovative ways of collaboration at all levels, in particular given the dynamism of its young civic societies. Europe should learn to adjust, no longer the other way around. European leaders should also bridge the vast gap between fine words about values, in public, and acts to the contrary, in the shadowy corridors of power. It would enhance their credibility.

An effort to achieve compatible political steering mechanisms should be a short-term objective. It would require streamlining between the capacities at the top levels focussed on policy strategy. The AU has a unit that is supposed to prepare and coordinate all its so-called strategic partnerships. In the EU at least two Commission directorates general and the EEAS jostle for control over external policies. A real innovation would be to create a joint policy strategy unit for the AU-EU Partnership in order to give it a central mind of governance. These are those cognitive functions and values which form the ingredients of effective policy-making in complex and adverse circumstances.

Serious questions must be raised to design a meaningful strategy. How can a supra- and international order, required by technology developments and business value chains, be combined with national democratic order? How can a common currency, such as the Euro, serve the common interest and not widen economic gaps? Is our ethical thinking up-to-date with the challenges of new sciences and technology? Can we align our views? Can we re-invent democracy to do it? And if the direction would be clear, despite the complexity and interdependence of current challenges, can we then innovate our governance systems rapidly and deeply enough to effectively fulfil its key functions of mentoring and monitoring societies and their markets, and to allocate capital in a way that primarily benefits the common good?

While this still leaves other asymmetries in the power structure, pragmatic steps can bring helpful tools, without in any way touching the existing legal and power structures. Soft arrangements are often preferable in international relations, at least they can help to develop alignment of direction and to improve understanding and trust.

Nevertheless Africa remains confronted with the current strategy design and implementation of the European External Action Service (EEAS) which since 2009 is at the heart of EU foreign relations and which was hoped to bring more coherence in the foreign actions of both the EU and its member states. It is still struggling to define its strategic mission, based on so-called common European values and on real economic and geopolitical interests (always prioritised), and it lacks the capacities for foresight, analysis and coherent implementation. Unconstructive frictions with the Commission are another permanent feature, not to mention ill-considered solo actions by member governments. The habit to set grand objectives and create new institutions without proper alignment of interests, without considering fracture points and without properly considering managerial consequences, is something European leaders share with African ones. But the AU Commission does not even have a similar body to coordinate.

The repeated EU proposal for an African Partnership could be a game change if the method could be to define the Partnership as an overarching EU mission, as the Commission is experimenting with in other areas, or as a comprehensive White Paper on the Relationship with Africa. The first is hindered because of the division of powers with EEAS, and the second because of an internal lack of consensus inside the Commission about the direction (in a nutshell: the clash between aid or trade vision).

Yet, it facilitates converging minds and practices to give an overarching policy direction with clearly defined objectives and framing of the various issues. As Mariana Mazzucato showed, missions require cross-disciplinary inputs and cross-sector collaboration by people with core and secondary competences, from different policy levels (EU, member states) and from the private sector (business, academia, civil society). They allow co-creation and complementary implementation by the various stakeholders, more flexible policy-making, avoiding the trap of a 'one-size-fits-all' approach in Unions with too diverse histories, views and interests. Regular dialogue mechanisms are required and objective feedback on the action undertaken. If the EEAS would give equal importance to horizontal (thematic) strategies as to geographic ones and formulate clear, long-term strategic objectives and priorities together, with more pragmatic short-term ones, and if these would be aligned with the policies and funding mechanisms of the Commission, and if the latter would define the Partnership as a Mission, there could be progress in practice. The synergy between various actions, and a coherent vision with a set of overarching objectives could emerge which can be understood and operationalised by both Europeans and Africans. Putting their own house in order would thus be a real practical contribution to developing a Partnership and facilitating the participation of the African governments in the process.

This leaves the problem of unanimity decision-making by the EU Foreign Ministers, as in the AU. It would of course be better to agree on a policy or an action with many than not to agree and not act at all and to create concrete successes which can spill over into other areas. The most resilient political groupings of the past were those which allowed diversity and space. But even then, the complexity on the EU side will not disappear and African governments, in order to create effective political leverage, would need to adjust their own foreign policy operating mechanisms. The most glaring deficiencies are the lack of efficacious coordination between the embassies of all AU countries in each EU member state, which would be a natural role for the AU Representation. But this one has limited capacities and political credibility and suffers from a lack of vision and leadership by the AU Commission. Africa has also a very weak presence in policy think tanks. The EU is driven by idealistic proposals and down-to-earth deals, and the first serve to prepare the second. Given the layered process of consensus building in the EU, at the national and EU level combined, these gaps weaken African governments significantly, while it would be relatively low cost to remedy it. African countries also have too little impact on Western media which present too often a one-sided image of these countries, thereby strengthening already existing prejudiced views.

In addition to such management reforms, more synergy between EU policies, programmes and funding mechanisms would help its efficacy, even though most of them remain stuck in an old paradigm and are in need of more radical reform. How can the EU promote a real Partnership with Africa, whose 54 countries all belong to the AU, but its main development cooperation is with north-Sahara countries which receive more funding than the rest of Africa, and when the EU Neighbourhood policy with the Mediterranean countries is designed in a different administrative silo? How can the EU aspire to connect its single market with a future African common market, if, at the same time, it continues to push, in addition to the post-Cotonou agreement, its European Partnership Agreements (EPA) with individual countries and with Africa's regional economic organisations (REC)? These are integral part of the AU system and could be a stepping stone for further integration, provided the EU would not seek to divide and rule; and provided EPA's with individual countries would not be signed because they risk splitting the RECs when other countries are not willing or ready to sign an EPA. They were once a useful response to the market fragmentation in Africa, but now, with the AfCFTA, they should fade into it or synergise with it, like pre-existing free trade treaties in Europe did after the Treaty of Rome came into full effect. How can the Commission define a coherent policy without setting a clear, overarching mission which binds all the Directorates-General together? Why is there no Commissioner for the Partnership? Not to mention reform in the EEAS. Ideally, but politically probably too difficult, there should be a process of parallel reforms in order to ensure more effective and fair cooperation.

CREATING A VIRTUOUS CYCLE

In the Museum of Art and Antiquities in Lisbon, there is a painting showing a large number of African traders in the port. Europeans have forgotten the role which Africans played in shaping their civilisation, but in the nineteenth century cultivated ignorance, with imperial purposes, pushed this sideways. There was once a mutually beneficial relationship and to restore it is today's grand mission. The AfCFTA requires a great deal more work, but it has all the potential to repeat the virtuous cycles which the Paris and Rome Treaties set in motion in Europe.

This European Commission wants to be a geopolitical one, because that is where many challenges to Europe's prosperity will be played out, and it wants to stimulate a rule-based, global order. But if one does not have a powerful global currency or sufficient military strength to make a difference, then a large market and funding a host of traditional aid programmes will be insufficient to exercise what is left: soft power. Soft power supposes that one has a societal model which is attractive to others and a narrative which speaks to people's hearts and minds. Europe's socially and ecologically corrected market economy certainly has that potential, because the essence of soft power is persuasion. But the exercise of soft power is a comprehensive exercise. It pre-supposes a fine-tuned understanding and appreciation of other people's historic pathways and the resulting, complex, cultural identities, of their state systems and societies. It is not something imperialist countries or technocratic structures naturally excel in, they often ignore so-called soft analysis from history or social sciences to complement the facts and figures; only together they can make evidence-based policies possible. A narrative that touches the hearts and minds of people, and symbolism, matters today as well, not least because of their easy spread via new media.

Many conditions need to be fulfilled for there to be equal partners. On the African side, the AfCFTA does not establish a supra-national, continental, legal entity like the EU with the power to conclude binding obligations on behalf of those members of the AU that have ratified the AfCFTA Agreement. It is a member-driven trade arrangement, which respects the national sovereignty of its members far more than the pooling of sovereignty in the EU. This also has consequences for the implementation of any agreements concluded, since it will be difficult to have a common court to hold member states to account. It is unclear how to resolve this conundrum. A Secretariat has been established but the strategic steering role of the AU Commission has been insufficiently clarified, and both lack capacities that member states are withholding, not unlike in Europe, where there is sometimes also a mismatch between grand political objectives and the capacities to implement them.

Another key problem is that AfCFTA provides for the continuation of the existing and partly overlapping regional economic communities (RECs). With one of them, SADC, the EU has been negotiating its Economic Partnership Agreements (EPAs), which are much contested in Africa. The AfCFTA envisages that tariffs and non-tariff barriers will be eliminated on the basis of variable geometry, which is fine on a bureaucratic drawing board, but not in corporate headquarters considering how to develop effective value chains. Since large corporations often act as a sort of locomotive for a host of small and medium-sized suppliers, this adds another design error from the start.

Other obstacles are formed by the EU and its Development Agreements with sub-Saharan countries, and different Neighborhood Agreements with north-Saharan countries, effectively dividing the African Union. As long as all funding is not channelled through a comprehensive AU-EU Partnership agreement, the EU effectively keeps dividing Sub-Saharan and north-Saharan countries, thus continuing the old colonial game. The key role of science and technology in the modern economy requires free trade in order to fully benefit from comparative advantages and the necessary scale.

When supporting the African initiative of a Common Free Trade Area, Europe should learn from its own successful experience, which brought prosperity back to its people, and operate similarly. The EU first of all needs a new conceptual view and a holistic and coherent approach to support this goal, backed up by sufficient and efficient funding.

The European Commission is often in a bend between vague vision, technocratic thinking and pious political wishes, though its new Global Gateway project and the organisation of Team Europe may herald a new beginning, provided that many framework conditions are put in place and that culture and management changes are stimulated in parallel. Europeans have started to re-discover their unsavoury past in Africa, but they limited the discussion to returning artefacts or removing statues, a clever way to divert attention from the real issues of inequality, continuing extraction and dependency, and from military intervention and support for dictatorships. Historians are setting the facts right. A new school of research has arisen to analyse the serious defects of development policies, which, despite the good intentions of many involved, did not bring structural transformations and did not shift the relationship into a more or less equitable one.

From an African perspective, there are only two other strategic partnerships possible at the moment: with the United States and with China. The harsh transactional capitalist market-driven approach of the first is no less upsetting to African social sensitivities than the harsh authoritarian centralism of the second. The US approach will lead to increasing inequalities and social tension; the Chinese one to the destruction of freedom and social bonds. Both are in essence neo-colonial and imperialist.

Despite all the criticism which can justifiably be levelled at it, the Europe model offers a middle way of a socially corrected market economy with a democratic political system and equality before the law. They probably respond best to Africa's civilisational roots and are conceptually sufficiently open to be adapted by Africans to suit their views and needs. However, if only European governments would practice abroad the values which they preach, it would be more convincing.

CHAPTER 7

Facing the Future

The writer James Baldwin has said that 'not everything that is faced can be changed, but nothing can be changed until it is faced'. This is true also for African-European interactions.

The only way for Europeans to make reparations for a distant past which they regret today, but for which they do not bear responsibility, is to face the current structural consequences of this past and to work together with Africans to overcome these. When the colonial states created by European colonial powers gained their legal sovereignty, they did not acquire at the same time the levers for economic self-determination. To build an equitable relationship, attention needs to be given now to remedying sociocultural identities and to upgrading economic resilience. It needs to touch the hearts and minds of people, as well as their living conditions.

History inevitably colours present minds and actions and it makes good diplomacy to take it fully into account. But it needs the victim's agreement and cooperation to be meaningful, it needs to respond to their sensitivities. Some heads of state have made a step in that direction but from a European perspective of offering regrets, which is a declaratory act, not one embedded in the victims' tradition and understanding. There are a few good examples in both continents, such as the French-German friendship treaty concluded after the second world war, or the Truth and

Reconciliation Council in South Africa after the end of apartheid. Historians and economists have been delving into the past and brought up the evidence. It should not remain limited to experts, it can be turned into new collective vision of the past, as a basis for moving on. It cannot change what happened long ago, but it can contribute to a better understanding as a new basis for jointly searching mutual beneficiation in the world of today. Close to each other, intertwined for centuries, Africans and Europeans have no choice but to try again, maybe fail again, and then try again and better.

A reset of the minds is a prerequisite for a strategic approach to cooperation. It needs an inclusive target, a clear pathway, a coherent set of tools and the capacity to use them. It requires agility in the face of volatile circumstances. It needs to be people centred. The African-European partnership idea could be the goal of an original comprehensive strategy, but one is still far away from it. A basket of projects inherited from the past is not an innovative strategy. It is a fake one.

The other big task lies in the economic domain. Of course, the EU and member states have been giving decades of development aid, but studies have shown that this had little impact on structural improvements. African economists have emphasised the essential need for structural transformation in agricultural and industrial sectors, to stimulate a sustainable economy capable of producing the goods and services which Africa wants and the world needs, to upgrade key economic inputs such as science and innovation, digitalisation or logistics, to help create the capacities and jobs for a rapidly growing population. Past policies, by African countries and self-centred Western donors, have failed to be transparent, and to bring timely structural transformations in line with global economic development and new ecological urgencies. The Eurocentric frame of minds also promoted only European models of governance and did not support efforts for modernising indigenous forms. The rule of law and human rights are essential, but other ways for consensual and responsible governance than the Western model can be imagined and tested.

No doubt there has been a lot of (superficial) goodwill, but at the same time there continues to be a lack of empathy and of deep understanding in EU decision-making circles, a dominance of short-term interest seeking and of the vested economic and/or political interests against the proclaimed European values and against radical innovation of vision and strategy. EU-Africa relations are still based on a postcolonial model, where Africa constitutes a commodities exporter, and current physical and other infrastructures fuel this role. Double standards continue to be applied. The well-meaning actions of individuals or companies cannot set a systemically wrong relationship right. Development policy has run into a dead end, it is an innovative trade policy that is needed for the relationship whereby available budgets are used for structural transformation, away from surviving economic colonialism. This can enhance the economic security and resilience of both groups of countries while maintaining openness for the benefits that trade had brought Africa during centuries.

This is matched by a lack of understanding of new European realities on the African side. Its media as well as its education systems, including its business schools, largely ignore Africa's main economic relationships. Authoritarian gerontocrats cleverly exploit this ignorance about contemporary Europe to wail about colonialism in order to hide their own lack of reforms. Worse, in order to get rid of the leftovers of European imperialism some turn to unrepented new imperialists which reintroduce military oppression and economic plunder. Africans often base their policy towards Europe on old thinking in Europe, which is fading away; in fact, new ideas are emerging already and only need to be nurtured, for example, alternative ways to handle free trade agreements and to manage collateral effects in societies. But this would require that they start engaging in the many think tanks and other circles for policy debate.

To bring better mutual insight, the EU could well design an African version of its successful Erasmus exchange programme, which has greatly contributed to bringing better mutual understanding among young Europeans who participated in it. It should be named after a great African thinker and be appropriate for the needs of African youth, on a large scale, not a pusillanimous extension of the existing one. Obviously, it should work also for European young people to get a real African experience.

But AU and EU do not yet succeed in designing an overarching and coherent framework, not for students, not for businesses from both continents, with a multitude of public-private partnerships in various sectors, and continue with the programme patchwork of the past and traditional development aid. The potential of African businesses and SMEs is often insufficiently appreciated. The role of African academia and research community is not fully included in European policy-making either. Policies that directly impact Africa are elaborated without real consultation, for example in, but not limited to, the agricultural and forestry domains. While most African migrants come to the EU lawfully—mainly through family reunion—there still is a stigma about them in many parts of Europe. The potential of the mutual diasporas (approx. 9 mio. of black Europeans and approx. 5 mio. of white Africans) still needs to be tapped.

The diplomatic compromise formulations of the February 2022 Summit cannot hide the apparent lack of alignment and lack of strategic vision and clear priorities, mainly caused by insufficient preparation, capacity shortages and institutional deficiencies, on both sides. As a result, the relationship remains asymmetric, there is no partnership of equals, and the conclusions lack operational clarity about the next steps. These summit conclusions seem more like a consolation prize.

New policies and radical amendments to existing ones, in particular the ACP and Mediterranean policies, are too slow in coming to deal efficaciously with rapidly changing geopolitical, economic and ecological conditions. The old and meanwhile discredited logic of development aid continues to hinder a focus on structural innovation, investment and trade. Short-term interests undermine long-term ones. Lack of policy synergy, coherent vision and appropriate ways of implementation make formidable obstacles to turn good intentions into effective innovative policy.

A system change is needed in the plethora of existing agreements. This was recognised by the Compact with Africa, but too many decision-makers and officials unimaginatively continue with old ways of thinking and outdated operations. The gap between word and deed remains wide. It will require leaving space for creativity and serendipity, but this is usually unwelcome in large intergovernmental organisations. An African Common Market will be greatly to the mutual benefit and all efforts should concentrate on helping it advance, taking into account Africa's regional diversities. To achieve the objectives of the AU Agenda 2063, it is essential to increase productive capacities in Africa for its growing markets for goods and services, which requires the creation of the proper framework conditions for investment and trade. Only fundamental redesign can make existing agreements fit for this purpose.

A future African-European Partnership can only live up to its proclaimed goals if political leaders are willing to put the quadruple goal of trade facilitation—investment facilitation—structural transformation—productive capacity growth at the core of its joint efforts. Climate neutrality and circular economy can be achieved through sharing green technology and digitalisation and through strengthening mutual research capacities. The EU's push for green industrialisation could have an

African pendant: instead of trading the required minerals in a neo-colonial fashion, African governments should insist on systematic industrialisation locally and on trading finished or half-finished products with Europe. Africans should resist a new resource grab and cooperate among themselves to set common terms and conduct joint negotiations with all those who need them. They should avoid being divided again. A majority of Europeans would like to see a new departure, a partnership of equals, only outdated views and agreements and some vested interests stand in the way. A process of deconstructing and replacing them is needed in both unions.

Sustainable industrialisation will undoubtedly contribute more than any other policy to peace and security and to reducing migratory pressures. However, it does require envisaging also compensatory mechanisms to deal with the collateral effects of trade liberation in Africa and with Europe, which are not all automatically positive for each country or each social group. The trade balance is far from beneficial for African countries.

It makes no sense to declare summit after summit grand objectives without ever discussing how to implement them. Independent evaluations are useful learning processes and can lead to continuous improvements; they are different from bureaucratic control of procedures and budgets because they need to involve stakeholders. New needs require new policies which require new governance organisation and innovative, digitalised management methods and increased capacities in Africa and in Europe. The asymmetries between the AU and EU institutions will be difficult to resolve, but ignoring them is no solution. Modern public management of the relationship's activities needs to be discussed openly, this surely can lead to incremental improvements as long as more fundamental ones are slow in coming, in particular on the African side where the new political elites have yet to come to terms that the colonial state systems which they inherited are out of date and require far more effective inter- and supranational mechanisms to deal with collective economic and ecological challenges.

Institutional change in inter-state organisations is extremely difficult and slow to realise, but people and climate cannot wait. Instead, a more pragmatic approach is needed by setting up coalitions of the willing on both continents.

One way to do so is to prepare jointly specific actions, in ad hoc jointly constituted groups of independent experts and stakeholders, who can then bring their proposals into the existing decision-making mechanism.

This would have the advantage of not hypothecating outcomes from the start by trying to fit everything into existing models, agreements and procedures. Europe cannot expect Africa to make amendments and avoid this process itself: it needs to include the changing economic and social dynamics in Africa, the growing primacy of the AU and the geopolitical alternatives for Africa in its own thinking and operations. Africans need to upgrade their acts in dealing with Europe, if they remain in a weak position there, they will also be weak in dealing with other economic powers and exploitation will continue.

Another practical option is to nominate in the Commission of AU and EU a member specifically tasked with designing and implementing a coherent strategy, bringing together the various bits now distributed in different silos. Their offices should be well funded and staffed with strategically thinking experts, which in turn should connect to the real world of citizens' organisations and business in both groups of countries. They could be the initiators of the dedicated expert groups proposed. A variant would be the method of a special negotiator, which was used successfully by the EU in the secession process of Great Britain.

African economists have written extensively about the needs of the continent and the way forward towards more prosperity for all. Usually, more or less the same priorities emerge: sustainable industrialisation, food production (preferably through regenerative agriculture) and health systems, energy, trade facilitation, funding, mutual cognitive and capacity improvement and governance modernisation. Too little attention is paid to how to achieve them. Public officials mostly prefer established, procedure focussed ways of carrying out their tasks; their political masters know that these kind of reforms produce results mostly after the next election when they are no longer seen as responsible for the outcome of what they set in motion. Public management modernisation experts are seldom involved. Independent evaluations are mostly avoided, and when they come from the academic or private sector, they are not seen as constructive contributions to change, but as unwanted criticism.

Synergy and policy cohesion are key problems to start with. The new so-called 'Team Europe' approach by the EU may bring improvements, on condition that it develops into a truly collaborative method and does away completely with development aid concepts. And this will not happen without an effort of common human resources retraining; Europe needs capacity training by Africa, though of a different kind than the capacity training offered to Africa. Europe can help to mobilise resources and create the framework conditions in a people-centred way by radically amending current cooperation programmes and designing creatively new ones, within a coherent strategic framework, with proper attention for interdependencies and collateral effects, in all realms which are essential for Africans to achieve similar conditions of welfare for all, as Europeans achieved during their industrialisation, partly through the use and abuse of African resources. The long-term consequences of colonialism risk having to distort economic, social and ecological effects now, also for Europe, so a systemic and enlightened new thinking, and new decision-making and implementation is needed. This will require political courage.

Rapidly growing populations in vast urban conglomerations, often as vulnerable as those in rural areas, demand a dual effort of building more quality housing and improving physical infrastructures. An upgrade of the digital infrastructure is needed for companies and for services to citizens. Together, these efforts can stimulate sustainable growth and massive job creation.

A multiplier effect can come about only through a coherent strategy linking investments in infrastructure, housing, energy and food systems. Environmental sustainability and climate neutrality are an investment to avoid future problems resulting from further climate deterioration and its economic and public health costs.

A holistic approach, based on the innovative concept of regenerative agriculture, is needed to sustainably increase productivity in African agriculture, to secure locally the food and medicines for more than 1 billion consumers, and to mitigate the effects of climate change. This will lift rural areas out of poverty and ensure the security of supply at affordable prices. Investments in rural areas must therefore be given a high priority. It will equally serve public health, provided the focus is on science-based and country-specific solutions.

Research and innovation, farmers' capacity acceleration, public-private partnerships and a strong and innovative financial sector are needed. This can be done in a national and regional context taking into account the vast ecological differences.

A vast array of jobs created through investments in industrialisation, housing and infrastructures will increase consumer purchasing of agricultural produce and help finance the improvement of the structural conditions for distribution and storage. Support for the African-specific sector strategies also requires remedying some distorting effects of the

EU's CAP and avoiding new ones as a result of the Farm to Fork strategy and the Green Deal. Overall, the conclusions of the UN Global Food Summit should be fully taken into account.

Sustainable forest management is necessary to ensure the multifunctional roles of forests for economic development in rural areas, for biodiversity and the development of biomaterials. The vast rain and dry forests, but also savannas and marshes in Africa play an important role in the fight against climate change through carbon sequestration. The time has come for the countries which emit more than the average CO_2 to reward those to absorb it, which in fact industrialised through massive deforestation themselves. The value of African forests for climate mitigation needs to be monetised, a demand which African governments should not hesitate to insist on. Rich country governments, with high climate-disturbing emissions, and corporations seeking to purchase carbon credit to offset continuing emissions, should pay for the conservation and management of forests. The system can ensure new employment for the people who are now forced to cooperate with deforestation. This requires also more attention to strengthening local research facilities and to facilitating access to new technologies to help with the sustainable use of land, reforestation and the multifunctional role of Africa's plantations.

The existing energy cooperation platform should enforce mechanisms for technology sharing with the EU green-tech sectors to stimulate Africa's transition to green energy, taking fully into account Africa's own, and different, pathway to climate neutrality, and equally supporting investments in African green start-ups and innovative enterprises. Hundreds of millions still have no access to electricity or to any other energy source than wood, they have therefore no alternative but deforestation and unproductive burning of it. Access everywhere to sustainable energy, an increase in production and distribution efficiency through digitalisation can be achieved with the aid of integrating energy markets. Renewable energy (in particular solar) can become a major source of supply for Africa, as well as for Europe. The transitory inclusion of nuclear and gas in the green category of Europe's taxonomy system will also facilitate Africa's access to finance to develop a mix of energy sources.

The key problem is how the people tasked with designing and implementing a new strategy can do so with the current limited capacities in both AU and EU. There are in fact three untapped resources: business, academia and civic society organisations. African-European cooperation is primarily a political-bureaucratic occupation, with weak roots in the 27 + 54 countries. Worse, the pretence of national policies to deal with such mega-issues itself undermines coherence and added value. Billions of European taxpayer money continue to be wasted, tens of millions of it end up in bank accounts in the money laundering centres of the world.

Structural changes in international organisations based on sovereign states are difficult to achieve. But it is easy to establish collaborative mechanisms which involve all stakeholders and which can both analyse the causes of persisting problems and creatively elaborate innovative proposals. This would require the EU to adjust its funding, in fact it would require just a fraction of the current development budget to help the operations of a multitude of such working groups. It is not done, because it would upset the vested interests of the white saviour industrial complex in Europe, and the kleptocratic mechanisms in Africa which feed on it.

Such joint, inclusive, sector-based and trans-sector groups can be helped by the use of professional foresight. This is not crystal ball gazing, but a trans-disciplinary method that seeks to improve the ability to anticipate, create and manage change in a variety of domains (scientific, technological, environmental, economic, cultural and societal), on a variety of scales (personal, organisational, societal, local, national and global) and through a variety of methods. The overarching objective is to permanently and comprehensively establish anticipatory thinking and a reflective handling of uncertainty in government institutions. It helps to bring changes in the culture of organisation and the processes of communication.

Foresight studies provide a solid launching platform for game-changing reform processes, in particular in settings where uncertainty resulting from complexity must be coped with and where a kaleidoscope of views and multiple, open and hidden, interests among different governance layers and non-state actors make the setting of policy direction very difficult, such as in the African-European context. They facilitate the development of a common framework of thinking and ultimately of alignment of policy vision and strategy elaboration. In political talk nowadays, how to deliver grand promises is often conveniently forgotten.

Of course, decision-makers may not like real consultation, which is organised scepticism. To tell voters 'there is no alternative' is comforting. Consultation and cooperation with stakeholders are not a cosmetic exercise, a benign one-off opportunity for stakeholders to vent their views when in fact the direction of policy and much of its elaboration is already decided and vested interests have been reassured. If properly executed, it can greatly contribute to the development of the quality and legitimacy of policy. It is a key ingredient in the accountability of decision-makers.

Collaborative governance needs formal organisation, ensuring that all stakeholders take part on equal footing and that there is clear progress towards a concrete outcome, being the setting of policy objectives, the outline of a regulatory architecture, or simply solving the practicalities in the invariably diverse realities.

The recent so-called Team Europe initiative seems to be a step in this direction. It implicitly recognised the weakness of the previous approach and seeks to mobilise the EU institutions, Member States and their Development Finance Institutions, the European Investment Bank, the European Bank for Reconstruction and Development, and the private sector behind common priorities in order to reach scale and create tangible and visible impact on the ground. However, it still falls short of a game change in policy-making and funding because it remains within established political-bureaucratic structures and procedures with too limited a role for economic and civic society actors from Africa. Despite the potential for a new dynamics, there is a risk of gradually being absorbed into the dominant paradigms.

The realisation of the AfCFTA will facilitate economic growth in all sectors and all countries and will increase employment opportunities. Trade facilitation should therefore be supported by all means and realised in the shortest possible time. All existing agreements should be brought in line with this overall objective. The EU should support the AU Commission with the strengthening of the AfCFTA Secretariat's capacities and operations.

The issue of non-tariff barriers remains important, not only because of quality standards but also because of tax and customs rules. There should be specific cooperation to deal with the former, through research, innovation and capacity acceleration. And there should be a mechanism to evaluate upfront the effects of the latter type of barriers, and to eliminate them if they are prohibitive, in particular on Africa's multitude of small and medium-sized enterprises.

Private sector capital can be forthcoming more easily with European public guarantees and by funding from existing, or future new dedicated financial institutions, but additional fragmentation must be avoided. Access to finance for start-ups and for SMEs needs to be facilitated to make the fit for production and innovation and for cooperation and integration in regional and global value chains. European support for domestic resource mobilisation in Africa should be strengthened, focussing on the use of digital technologies, effective taxation and eliminating European tax on remittances from Africans working in Europe.

Implementation requires special attention to capacity acceleration in the public and private sectors in Europe and in Africa, by stimulating research, training and apprenticeships, engaging universities, business schools and think tanks and institutes of public administration and management, and by strengthening Africa's own research facilities to support innovation in all economic sectors, and to the creation of regional food safety agencies, environmental protection agencies and others relevant for modern society. Start-ups and scale-ups should receive specific support to grow.

Governance capabilities to implement the Partnership strategy need to be upgraded and extended in both Africa and Europe in line with its objectives. The AU and EU must be re-made to be fit for the purpose in the emerging future global geopolitical, economic and ecological circumstances. Both the AU and EU are inter-state organisations which are in constant need of management modernisation and learning processes to deal with complex and relentless problems which were not foreseen at the time of their establishment.

Nothing can be done without the involvement of business, civic societies and academia. African-European cooperation must therefore move beyond a state and public sector-based focus and design open sector-specific and coherent frameworks within which all can contribute to the goals set. Truly mutual consultation, mutual agenda setting and annually independent evaluation (involving stakeholders) of the progress in implementing this roadmap are a must.

The institutional asymmetries must be dealt with. An expert group could be tasked with elaborating possible solutions, but in the short term a pragmatic, collaborative approach can assist with setting up new joint groups, including business and civic society, to elaborate proposals and oversee implementation for all relevant issues. But there is another realm for action, the social-cultural. European countries need to face up the uncomfortable reality of the past. History telling cannot just focus on the positive sides of industrialisation, on the welfare which it has brought and the improvement in living conditions, unparalleled in history. There were dark sides: labour exploitation, ecological destruction, and colonial exploitation. The first has been recognised, thanks to enlightened and socially minded people and actions by workers themselves. The second is being dealt with finally, because the negative effects for all could no longer be ignored. The third is still in need of objective assessment and recognition.

Economic value creation starts from demand. This can come from the needs of industry to find solutions to specific problems in their value chain (such as resource efficiency) or from continuously emerging and changing societal needs (such as quality of living). Innovation will also come often through the involvement of stakeholders (co-creation). African forests, or traditional African food products, and nearly all extractions from Africa's rich soil and waters offer great potential for multiple value creation, but they are among the many opportunities hitherto neglected because of too European research perspectives.

Demand-driven value creation implies ensuring permanent strategic agility, scanning the global context, scouting for opportunities, and attention to continuities or discontinuities. The emergence of novel concepts or processes, products or services, is often the result of out-of-the-box thinking, improvisation, repeated trial and error and the emergence of new tacit and explicit knowledge until some form of consolidation takes place. This is where the education system reforms and capacity upgrading and acceleration comes in.

African governments need to reconnect their modern education systems from colonial times with their ancient wisdom and learnings, but both they and the Europeans should clean up their history books to ensure that future generations learn a balanced history about their nineteenth and twentieth centuries. This will require bringing new historic knowledge from the experts' circles into the mainstream of teaching. This will take time to produce effect, but meanwhile, the public media should be pushed to offer a more equitable view of each other. European media still offer too often an image of Africa that maintains colonial stereotypes and pass over the dynamism of their modern societies. There is a need for Europe to help build African news agencies in order to bring more balance and objectivity in reporting from Africa to the rest of the world.

Europe has been helping Africa for years with capacity-building programmes, but there has seldom been an objective evaluation of their impact, probably for good reasons. It would be far more advantageous for Africa to focus European support on its universities and business schools. New knowledge would be institutionalised and blended with local conditions and expertise, and thus have a more permanent impact. The importance of human capital for structural transformation stems from how skilled people generate new knowledge, contribute to adapting existing technologies and ideas, and from spillovers of human capital between workers.

What is required are innovative, holistic learning systems blending theory with practice and focussing on leadership development at all stages. Capacity acceleration for product or service innovation in view of changes in the market is needed urgently for Africa's approximately half a million or more SMEs, which can be nurtured to make a gazelle jump to transform the economy. It should be coupled with an understanding of opportunities and risks for business within the new trade framework created by the AfCFTA. A transformative mindset with the large corporations operating in Africa, whatever their origin, will facilitate their roles as locomotives. But this will not come automatically, it needs an effort of innovative leadership development through Africa's business schools.

In addition, the EU should finance extensive, two-way student and youth exchange programmes (inspired by the successful EU Erasmus Exchange programme and proportionally of the same size), research and think tanks cooperation, strengthening cooperation between civil society organisations, assistance in (re-)building Africa's cultural infrastructures, which requires more effort than just returning some artworks.

The widespread cognitive gaps about earlier comprehensive relations between both continents since Roman times must be addressed, as well as the positive roles which trade with Africa played in Europe's own development and culture. Without change, these often-hidden views and sentiments will continue to hypothecate the engagement of stakeholders and decision-makers alike for another generation.

Throughout history, geography has determined that European and African countries are neighbours. For centuries, this was a fair and equitable relationship, until the time of industrialisation and its accompanying colonialism, the consequences of which are felt till today. Old structures and top-down forms of bureaucratic cooperation need to be cleared away. The forces of civic society and of entrepreneurs in Africa and Europe need to become better connected. The focus must shift to structural transformation, away from neo-colonial aid and development. The minds must be cleared of discredited ideas about each other. A comprehensive friendship agreement with concrete objectives and means attached, is needed as a concrete follow-up of acts of forgiveness. Africa is rising, and Europe should stand on its side this time, in the mutual short and long-term interest, and to be true to proclaimed humanitarian values. But above all, enlightened people in both continents should remember that the dialectics of markets and actions of civil societies constitute the prime historic forces for change.

Bibliography

Foreword

Ba, Sylvia Washington, *The Concept of Negritude in the Poetry of Leopold Sedar Senghor*, Princeton University Press, 2016.
Margalit, Avishai, *The Ethics of Memory*, Cambridge, Massachusetts: Harvard University Press, 2004.
Otele, Olivette, *African Europeans: An Untold History*, London: Basic Books, 2022.
Senghor, Leopold S., *Leopold Sedar Senghor: The Collected Poetry*, University of Virginia Press, 1998.

Chapter 1: Introduction

Ba, Sylvia Washington, *The Concept of Negritude in the Poetry of Leopold Sedar Senghor*, Princeton University Press, 2016.
Frobenius, Leo, *Die Geheimbünde Afrikas*, Hamburg, Germany, 1894.
Frobenius, Leo, *Weltgeschichte des Krieges*, Hannover, Germany, 1903.
Frobenius, Leo and Fox, D. Claughton, *African Genesis*, Stockpile Sons, 1937.
Frobenius, Leo, edited by Haberland, Eike and foreword by Senghor, Leopold S. (Foreword), *Leo Frobenius on African History, Art and Culture*, Markus Wiener Publishers, 2014.
Irwin, Robert, *Dangerous Knowledge*, Woodstock and New York: The Overlook Press, 2006.

Kuba, Richard, "The Expeditions of Leo Frobenius between Science and Politics: Nigeria 1910–1912", in BEROSE- *International Encyclopaedia of the Histories of Anthropology*, Paris, 2020.

Mbeki, Moeletsi, *Architects of Poverty*, Picador Africa, South Africa, 2009.

Said, W. Edward, *Orientalism*, Pantheon Books, 1978.

Said, W. Edward, *Culture and Imperialism*, Chatto & Windus, 1993.

Senghor, Leopold S., *Leopold Sedar Senghor: The Collected Poetry*, University of Virginia Press, 1998.

Chapter 2: Pre-Colonial Political Order in Africa

Andrews, E., *7 Influential African Empires—History*, History Stories. HISTORY.com. Available at: https://www.history.com/news/7-influential-african-empires (no date).

Arkwell, A., *A History of the Sudan to 1821*, Athlone Press, 1961.

BBC (2022), *What Was Precolonial West Africa Like? BBC Bitesize*. BBC. Available at: https://www.bbc.co.uk/bitesize/topics/zj4fn9q/articles/zs4ptrd, Black History Month, 2019.

BBC (2023), *The History of the Kingdom of Dahomey*, Black History Month. Available at: https://www.blackhistorymonth.org.uk/article/section/pre-colonial-history/the-history-of-the-kingdom-of-dahomey/, 2023.

BBC World Service (n.d.). *The Story of Africa* [online]. www.bbc.co.uk. Available at: https://www.bbc.co.uk/worldservice/africa/features/storyofafrica/4chapter2.sht, 2023.

Black Demographics, *African American Ancestry: The Akan States of the Gold Coast* [online]. Blackdemographics.com. Available at: https://blackdemographics.com/african-american-ancestry-the-akan-states-of-the-gold-coast/, 2019.

Black History Month, *The Kingdom of Kush*, Black History Month [on creative license]. Available at: https://www.blackhistorymonth.org.uk/article/section/pre-colonial-history/3781/, 2019.

Boissoneault, L., *The Golden Age of Timbuktu* [online]. JSTOR Daily. Available at: https://daily.jstor.org/golden-age-timbuktu/, 2018.

Bovill, E.W., *The Golden Trade of the Moors*, Oxford University Press, 1957.

Budge, E.A. Wallis, *A History of Ethiopia*, 2 vols, London: Methuen, 1928.

Cartwright, M., *Mapungubwe* [online]. World History Encyclopedia. Available at: https://www.worldhistory.org/Mapungubwe/, 2019.

Cartwright, M., *Kingdom of Abyssinia* [online]. World History Encyclopedia. Available at: https://www.worldhistory.org/Kingdom_of_Abyssinia/, 2019.

Cartwright, M., *Mutapa* [online]. World History Encyclopedia. Available at: https://www.worldhistory.org/Mutapa/, 2019.

Cartwright, M. *Mali Empire* [online]. Humanities—LibreTexts. Available at: https://human.libretexts.org/Courses/Arapahoe_Community_College/World_Mythology_(Stafinbil)_;_Under_Construction/09%3A_Africa_(excluding_Egypt)/9.02%3A_Mali_Empire, 2021.
Collins, Robert O., *The Precolonial Centuries*, Princeton: Markus Wiener Publishers, 2014.
Chimee, I.N., *African Historiography and the Challenges of European Periodization: A Historical Comment* [online]. TRAFO—Blog for Transregional Research. Available at: https://trafo.hypotheses.org/11518, 2018.
Crummey, D.E. *Ethiopia—Federal Democratic Republic of Ethiopia* [online]. Encyclopædia Britannica. Available at: https://www.britannica.com/place/Ethiopia/Federal-Democratic-Republic-of-Ethiopia.
Davidson, Basil, *The Lost Cities of Africa*, Pollinger, 1959.
Davidson, Basil, *The African Past*, London: Longmans, 1964.
de Prorok, Byron Kuhn, "Ancient Trade Routes from Carthage into the Sahara", in *Geographical Review*, Vol 15, No 2, 1925.
Epic World History (n.d.). *Epic World History: Akan States of West Africa* [online]. Epic World History Blog. Available at: http://epicworldhistory.blogspot.com/2012/07/akan-states-of-west-africa.html, 2023.
Fiola, Toyin, *Decolonizing African Knowledge: Autoethnography and African Epistemologies*, UK: Cambridge, USA, New York, NY: Cambridge University Press, 2022.
Foster, H.J. "The Ethnicity of the Ancient Egyptians", in *Journal of Black Studies*, Vol 5, No 2, pp. 175–191, 1974.
Green, T., *A Fistful of Shells: West Africa from the Rise of the Slave Trade to the Age of Revolution*, London, UK: Penguin, 2019.
Green, T., *Liberating the Precolonial History of Africa: Aeon Essays, Africa, in Its Fullness*. Edited by S. Haselby. Aeon Magazine. Available at: https://aeon.co/essays/liberating-the-precolonial-history-of-africa, 2021.
Gryc, W., *Book Review: The Evolution of Civilizations* [online]. 10 Million Steps. Available at: https://10millionsteps.com/review-evolution-of-civilizations, 2019.
Havard Divinity School (n.d.). *Sokoto Caliphate* [online]. rpl.hds.harvard.edu. Available at: https://rpl.hds.harvard.edu/faq/sokoto-caliphate.
Heritage Daily, *The Kingdom of Zimbabwe* [online]. Heritage Daily—Archaeology News. Available at: https://www.heritagedaily.com/2020/04/the-kingdom-of-zimbabwe/119738?amp, 2020.
Hodgkin, T. (n.d.). *Usman dan Fodio | Fulani leader* [online]. www.britannica.com. Available at: https://www.britannica.com/biography/Usman-dan-Fodio.
HomeTeam History, *What Were Africans Doing in 1492? YouTube*. Available at: https://www.youtube.com/watch?v=oCqMjSKxPHM, 2019

Hunt, P., "Carthage", in *Encyclopædia Britannica* [online]. Available at: https://www.britannica.com/place/Carthage-ancient-city-Tunisia, 2021.

Kazora, B., *The Great Empires and Kingdoms of Pre-Colonial and Pre-Slavery African*. Available at: https://benkazora.medium.com/the-great-empires-and-kingdoms-of-pre-colonial-and-pre-slavery-african-7fe57321cac0, 2021.

Khan, S.M., *Ottoman Empire* [online]. World History Encyclopedia. Available at: https://www.worldhistory.org/Ottoman_Empire/, 2020.

Kiwanuka, M.S.M., "African Pre-Colonial History: A Challenge to the Historian's Craft", in *Journal of Eastern African Research & Development*, Vol 2, No 1, pp. 69–77, 1972.

Lawton, B., *Sankore Mosque and University (c. 1100)* [online]. Black Past. Available at: https://www.blackpast.org/global-african-history/institutions-global-african-history/sankore-mosque-and-university-c-1100/, 2020.

Manning, S., *Britain at War with the Asante Nation, 1823–1900: "The White Man's Grave"*, Pen & Sword Books, 2021.

Marcus, H.G. and Anthony Low, D. "Eastern Africa", in *Encyclopædia Britannica* [online]. Available at: https://www.britannica.com/place/eastern-Africa, 2015.

Mark, J.J., *Punt* [online]. World History Encyclopedia. Available at: https://www.worldhistory.org/punt/, 2011.

Mark, J.J., *Carthage* [online]. World History Encyclopedia. Available at: https://www.worldhistory.org/carthage/, 2020.

Marks, S., "Southern Africa", in *Encyclopædia Britannica* [online]. Available at: https://www.britannica.com/place/Southern-Africa, 2019.

Mhango, N.N., *How Africa Developed Europe: Deconstructing the History of Africa, Excavating Untold Truth and What out to be Done and Known*, Bamenda, Cameroon: Langaa Research & Publishing CIG, 2018.

Michael, B. (n.d.). *Queen Yodit/Gudit* [online]. allaboutETHIO. Available at https://allaboutethio.com/hjudith.html, 2023.

Michalopoulos, S. and Papaioannou, E., "Historical Legacies and African Development", in *Journal of Economic Literature* Vol 58, No 1, pp. 53–128, 2020.

Mohamud, N., "Is Mansa Musa the Richest Man Who Ever Lived?", in *BBC News* [online]. 10 March Available at: https://www.bbc.co.uk/news/world-africa-47379458, 2019.

National Geographic Education (n.d.), "Carthage", [online]. National Geographic Society. Available at: https://education.nationalgeographic.org/resource/carthage/.

National Geographic Education (n.d.). *Sundiata Keita* [online]. education.nationalgeographic.org. Available at: https://education.nationalgeographic.org/resource/sundiata-keita/, 2023.

National Geographic Education (n.d.). *Key Components of Civilization* [online]. education.nationalgeographic.org. Available at: https://education.nationalgeographic.org/resource/key-components-civilization/, 2023.

Nnoromele, S., and Anyanwu, O.E., *Re-tracing Africa; A Multi-Disciplinary Study of African History, Societies and Culture*. Dubuque, IA: Kendall Hunt, 2015.

Oliver, Roland and Fage, D.J., *A Short History of Africa*, London, UK: Penguin, 1963.

Olusoga, D., *First Contacts: The Cult of Progress*, Profile Books Limited, 2018.

Pike, J., *Sokoto Caliphate* [online]. Globalsecurity.org. Available at: https://www.globalsecurity.org/military/world/nigeria/sokoto.htm, 2022.

Rob, A., *Black Histories: Oba Ewuare & Benin City, Black History Month*. Available at: https://www.blackhistorymonth.org.uk/article/section/pre-colonial-history/black-histories-oba-ewuare-benin-city/, 2015.

Schepers, S., "Ubuntu and the European Welfare State Model", in *The Thinker*, Vol 67, 2016.

Shinnie, M., *Ancient African Kingdoms*, London: St Martins Press, 1958.

South African History Online, *Kingdoms of Southern Africa: Mapungubwe* [online]. South African History Online. Available at: https://www.sahistory.org.za/article/kingdoms-southern-africa-mapungubwe, 2018.

Spearman, D., *Brief History of Africa Before Colonialism—How Did We Get There? YouTube*. Available at: https://www.youtube.com/watch?v=wHrGorccjcg, 2020.

The British Museum, *Benin Bronzes, The British Museum*. Available at: https://www.britishmuseum.org/about-us/british-museum-story/contested-objects-collection/benin-bronzes (no date).

The Editors of Encyclopaedia Britannica, "Songhai Empire | History, Facts, & Fall", in [online]. *Encyclopædia Britannica*. Available at: https://www.britannica.com/place/Songhai-empire (no date).

The Editors of Encyclopaedia Britannica, "Akan States", in [online]. *Encyclopedia Britannica*. Available at: https://www.britannica.com/place/Akan-states (no date).

The Editors of Encyclopaedia Britannica, "Mwene Matapa | Historical Dynastic Title, Southern Africa", in [online]. *Encyclopedia Britannica*. Available at: https://www.britannica.com/topic/Mwene-Matapa (no date).

The Editors of Encyclopaedia Britannica (n.d.). "Punt", in [online]. *Encyclopedia Britannica*. Available at: https://www.britannica.com/place/Punt-historical-region-Africa (no date).

The Editors of Encyclopedia Britannica, "Mali: Historical Empire, Africa", in [online]. *Encyclopædia Britannica*. Available at: https://www.britannica.com/place/Mali-historical-empire-Africa, 2019.

Think Africa Editorial Team, "Kingdom of Zimbabwe (1220–1450 AD)", in [online]. *Think Africa*. Available at: https://thinkafrica.net/zimbabwe/, 2018.

Think Africa Editorial Team, "Land of Punt (Pwnt)-Land of the Gods", in [online]. *Think Africa*. Available at: https://thinkafrica.net/land-of-punt/, 2018.

Timberg, C. and Halperin, D., "Colonialism in Africa Helped Launch the HIV Epidemic a Century Ago", in [online]. *Washington Post*. Available at: https://www.washingtonpost.com/national/health-science/colonialism-in-africa-helped-launch-the-hiv-epidemic-a-century-ago/2012/02/21/gIQAyJ9aeR_story.html, 2012.

Toit, M.D., *9 Ancient African Kingdoms You Should Know About, Rhino Africa Blog*. Available at: https://blog.rhinoafrica.com/2018/03/27/9-ancient-african-kingdoms/, 2018.

Quigley, Carroll, *Evolution of Civilizations*, London: Macmillan, 1961.

Understanding Slavery, *Africa Before Transatlantic Enslavement, Black History Month*. Available at: https://www.blackhistorymonth.org.uk/article/section/history-of-slavery/africa-before-transatlantic-enslavement/, 2021.

UNESCO World Heritage Centre, "Mapungubwe Cultural Landscape", in [online]. *UNESCO World Heritage Centre*. Available at: https://whc.unesco.org/en/list/1099/ (no date).

UNESCO.org, "UNESCO—Manden Charter, Proclaimed in Kurukan Fuga", in [online]. ich.unesco.org. Available at: https://ich.unesco.org/en/RL/manden-charter-proclaimed-in-kurukan-fuga-00290 (no date).

Waweru, N., "This Badass Queen Took Revenge on Ethiopia in 960 AD for Chopping off Her Breasts", in [online]. *Face2Face Africa*. Available at: https://face2faceafrica.com/article/this-badass-queen-took-revenge-on-ethiopia-in-960-ad-for-chopping-off-her-breasts, 2018.

Chapter 3: Pillars of Africa's Ancient Economies

de Prorok, Byron Kuhn, "Ancient Trade Routes from Carthage into the Sahara", in *Geographical Review*, Vol 15, No 2, 1925.

Farrar, T., *Precolonial African Material Culture: Combatting Stereotypes of Technological Backwardness*, Lanham, Maryland: Lexington Books, 2020.

Goswami, C.R., 2003, January. Professor PS Gupta Prize Essay: "The Slave Trade at Zanzibar and the Role of Kutchis", in *Proceedings of the Indian History Congress* (Vol. 64, pp. 1281–1294). Indian History Congress.

Green, T., *A Fistful of Shells: West Africa from the Rise of the Slave Trade to the Age of Revolution*, London, UK: Penguin, 2003.

July, R.W., *Precolonial Africa: An Economic and Social History*, New York: Scribner, 1975.

Kusimba, C.M., "Archaeology of Slavery in East Africa", in *African Archaeological Review*, Vol 21, No 2, pp. 59–88, 2004.

Michalopoulos, S., *Historical Legacies and African Development*, Cambridge, MA: National Bureau of Economic Research, November 2018.

Ndee, H.S., "Pre-Colonial East Africa: History, Culture and Physical Activity", in *The International Journal of the History of Sport*, Vol 27, No 5, pp. 780–797, 2010.

Piketty, Thomas, *Capital in the Twenty-First Century*, Belknap Press, 2014.

Piketty, Thomas, *Une brève histoire de l'égalité*, Paris Ed. du Seuil, 2021.

Piketty, Thomas, *A Brief History of Equality*, Belknap Press, 2022.

Sheriff, A.H., "The Dynamics of Change in Pre-Colonial East African Societies", in *African Economic History Review* Vol 1, No 2, pp. 7–14, 1974.

The Colonial Williamsburg Foundation, "Transatlantic Slave Trade", in [online]. *The Colonial Williamsburg Foundation*. Available at: http://slaveryandremembrance.org/articles/article/?id=A0002, 2019.

Understanding Slavery, *Africa Before Transatlantic Enslavement—Black History Month 2019* [online]. Black History Month 2019. Available at: https://www.blackhistorymonth.org.uk/article/section/history-of-slavery/africa-before-transatlantic-enslavement/, 2019.

Van Bavel, B.J. and van Bavel, B., *The Invisible Hand? How Market Economies Have Emerged And Declined Since AD 50*, UK: Oxford University Press, 2016.

Chapter 4: African Pre-Colonial Social and Political Structures

Ayittey, G., *Indigenous African Institutions*. Brill, 2006.

Berg-Schlosser, D., "African Political Systems: Typology and Performance", in *Comparative Political Studies*, Vol 17, No 1, pp. 121–151, 1984.

Biswas, S., " Communitarianism: Definitions, History, Features, Communitarians", in [online]. *Sociology Group: Sociology and Other Social Sciences Blog*. Available at: https://www.sociologygroup.com/communitarianism/, 2021.

Eldredge, E.A., "Pre-colonial Political Institutions: Relevance for Contemporary Africa", in Oloruntoba, S., Falola, T. (eds.), *The Palgrave Handbook of African Politics, Governance and Development*, New York: Palgrave Macmillan, 2018.

Eleojo, Egbunu F., "Africans and African Humanism: What Prospects?", in the *American International Journal of Contemporary Research*, Vol 4, No 1, March 2014.

Elhanafy, H. and Olawoye, E. *City-States as a Cornerstone for Pre-Colonial Urban Development* [online]. Charter Cities Institute. Available at: https://chartercitiesinstitute.org/blog-posts/building-africa-city-states-as-a-cornerstone-for-pre-colonial-urban-development-in-africa/, 2020.

Eze, O.C., Omeje, P.U. and Chinweuba, U.G., "The Igbo: A Stateless Society", in the *Mediterranean Journal of Social Sciences*, Vol 5, No 27, P3, p. 1315, 2014.

Fakuade, O., "Stateless Societies: The Igbo, the Fulani, the Somali" by Prof G.N Ayittey, in [online] *A New Nigeria*. Available at: https://seunfakze.wordpress.com/2012/02/21/stateless-societies-the-igbo-the-fulani-the-somali-by-prof-g-n-ayittey/, 2012.

Fisseha, M., "The Rise of Feudalism in Ethiopia", in [online] *Ethiopian Business Review*. Available at: https://ethiopianbusinessreview.net/the-rise-of-feudalism-in-ethiopia/#:~:text=In%20Ethiopian%2C%20feudalism%20was%20institutionalized, 2018.

Goody, Jack, *The East in the West*, UK: Cambridge University Press, 2012.

Hofsteede, Geert, *Cultures and Organisations*, McGraw-Hill, 1991.

Jefferson, T., "From Thomas Jefferson to Edward Carrington, 16 January 1787", in [online]. *Founders Online*. Available at: https://founders.archives.gov/documents/Jefferson/01-11-02-0047

John, R., *Africa: A Biography of the Continent*, Penguin UK, 1997.

Johnson, E.O., "5 Ancient African Social Structures That Thrived Before Colonisers Imposed Western Versions" Page 3 of 6, in [online]. *Face2Face Africa*. Available at: https://face2faceafrica.com/article/5-ancient-african-social-structures-that-thrived-before-colonisers-imposed-western-versions/3, 2018.

Johnson, E.O., "This African King Ruled Over a Democratic Nation Centuries Before Abraham Lincoln", in [online] *Face2Face Africa*. Available at: https://face2faceafrica.com/article/this-african-king-ruled-over-a-democratic-nation-centuries-before-abraham-lincoln, 2018.

Management Study Guide, "The Political System—Meaning and Concept", in [online] *Management Study Guide*. Available at: https://www.managementstudyguide.com/political-system.ht (no date).

Mandela, Nelson, *Long Walk to Freedom*, Little Brown & Company, 1994.

Michalopoulos S., and Papaioannou, E., "Pre-Colonial Ethnic Institutions and Contemporary African Development", in *Econometrica*, Vol 81, No 1, pp 113–152, 2013.

Mills, W.G., *Stateless Societies*, on [online]. Saint Mary's University, Canada. Available at: http://smu-facweb.smu.ca/~wmills/course316/11Nuer.html (no date).

Nunn, N., Robinson, J. and Moscona, J., "Social Structure and Conflict in sub-Saharan Africa", in [online] *Centre for Economic Policy Research*. Available at: https://cepr.org/voxeu/columns/social-structure-and-conflict-sub-saharan-africa, 2018.

Palagashvili, L., "African Chiefs: Comparative Governance Under Colonial Rule", in *Public Choice*, Vol 174, No (3–4), pp. 277–300, 2018.

Parsons, Talcott, *The Structure of Social Action*, The Free Press, 1967.
Parsons, Talcott, *The Social System*, Psychology Press, 1991.
Said, W. Edward, *Orientalism*, Pantheon Books, 1978.
Said, W. Edward, *Culture and Imperialism*, Chatto & Windus, 1993.
Samuel-Mbaekwe, I.J., "Colonialism and Social Structure", in *Transafrican Journal of History*, Vol 15, pp. 81–95, 1986.
Study.com, "Social Systems: Definition & Theory", in [online] Study.com. Available at: https://study.com/academy/lesson/social-systems-definition-theory-quiz.htm, 2020.
Taylor, S., "Hidden Black History: 7 African Queens Who Have Made Their Mark", in [online] *Ebony*. Available at: https://www.ebony.com/7-african-queens-history/, 2022.
The Editors of Encyclopaedia Britannica, "Chiefdom", in *Encyclopædia Britannica* [online]. Available at: https://www.britannica.com/topic/chiefdom, 2019.
Think Africa Editorial Team, "Africa's 15 Pre-Colonial Political Systems", in [online]. *Think Africa*. Available at: https://thinkafrica.net/africas-15-pre-colonial-political-systems/, 2019.
Tosh, J., "Colonial Chiefs in a Stateless Society: A Case-Study from Northern Uganda", in *The Journal of African History*, Vol 14, No 3, pp. 473–490, 1973.
Utin, I.B., "Political Systems and Underdevelopment in Africa (1957–2010)", in *AFRREV IJAH: An International Journal of Arts and Humanities*, Vol 7, No 2, pp 8–15, 2018.

CHAPTER 5: COLONIALISM AND THE STRUGGLE FOR INDEPENDENCE

Aldcroft, D., and Morewood, S., *The European Economy Since 1914* (1st ed.). Routledge, 2012.
Ba, Sylvia Washington, *The Concept of Negritude in the Poetry of Leopold Sedar Senghor*, Princeton University Press, 2016.
BBC World Service, *The Story of Africa* [online]. www.bbc.co.uk. Available at: https://www.bbc.co.uk/worldservice/africa/features/storyofafrica/4chapter2.shtml (no date).
Césaire, Aimé, *Discourse on Colonialism*, Paris: Éditions Réclame, 1950.
De Goede, M., *An analysis of Mahmood Mamdani's Citizen and Subject*, London: Macat, 2017.
Diouf, K., "Why No African Country Is Truly Free or Independent", on [online] *The African Courier*. Available at: https://www.theafricancourier.de/news/africa/neo-colonialism-in-africa-the-illusion-of-freedom/, 2020.

Easterly, W., "Don't Say Colonialism! The Debate on Paul Collier", on [online] *Aid Watch Blog*. Available at: https://www.nyudri.org/aidwatcharchive/2009/07/don%E2%80%99t-say-colonialism-the-debate-on-paul-collier, 2009.

France 24, *1960: A Wave of Independence Sweeps Across Africa* [online]. France 24. Available at: https://www.france24.com/en/20200709-1960-a-wave-of-independence-sweeps-across-africa, 2020.

Frankel, S.H., "Economic Aspects of Political Independence in Africa", in *International Affairs (Royal Institute of International Affairs 1944-)*, Vol 36, No 4, pp. 440–446, 1960.

Gathara, P. "Eurafrica and the Myth of African Independence", on [online]. *Aljazeera*. Available at: https://www.aljazeera.com/opinions/2019/11/24/eurafrica-and-the-myth-of-african-independence, 2019.

Gregory, S., "The French military in Africa: Past and Present", in *African Affairs*, Vol 99, No 396, pp. 435–448, 2000.

Hansen, Peo, and Jonsson, S., *Building Eurafrica: Reviving Colonialism Through European Integration, 1920–1960*, 2011.

Hansen, Peo, and Johnson, Stefan, *EurAfrica: The Untold History of European Integration and Colonialism*, London and New York: Bloomsbury, Academic, 2014.

Hewson, M., "Review of The Origins of Political Order: From Prehuman Times to the French Revolution", in *Reviews in History*. Available at: https://reviews.history.ac.uk/review/1261, 2012.

History.com Editors, "Marshall Plan", in [online] *History*. Available at: https://www.history.com/topics/world-war-ii/marshall-plan-1#:~:text=The%20Marshall%20Plan%2C%20also%20known, 2009.

Khapoya, V., *The African Experience*. Routledge, 2015.

Kieh, G.K., "Neo-colonialism: American Foreign Policy and the First Liberian Civil War", in *The Journal of Pan African Studies*, Vol 5, No 1, pp. 164–184, 2012.

Kohn, M. and Reddy, K., "Colonialism", in [online]. *Stanford Encyclopedia of Philosophy*. Available at: https://plato.stanford.edu/entries/colonialism/, 2017.

Kotsopoulos, J., "Can the Relationship Between Europe and Africa Stand the Test of Time?" in [online]. *The Conversation*. Available at: https://theconversation.com/can-the-relationship-between-europe-and-africa-stand-the-test-of-time-75136, 2017.

Marks, S.E., "Southern Africa—Independence and Decolonization in Southern Africa", in [online]. *Encyclopædia Britannica*. Available at: https://www.britannica.com/place/Southern-Africa/Independence-and-decolonization-in-Southern-Africa, 2014.

Moyd, M., "Resistance and Rebellions (Africa)", in [online]. *1914–1918: International Encyclopedia of the First World War*, 2017.

Murray, A.D., *The Development of the Alternative Black Curriculum, 1890–1940: Countering the Master Narrative*, Cham, Switzerland: Palgrave Macmillan, 2018.

Nylander, F., "The Legacy of Colonialism: The Shadow of French Uranium Mines", in [online] *African Apocalypse*. Available at: https://africanapocalypsefilm.com/finding-a-way-from-french-uranium-mines-to-harnessing-the-power-of-the-sun/, 2020.

Piketty, Thomas, *Capital in the Twenty-First Century*, Belknap Press, 2014.

Piketty, Thomas, *Une brève histoire de l'égalité*, Paris Ed. du Seuil, 2021.

Piketty, Thomas, *A Brief History of Equality*, Belknap Press, 2022.

Rupp, G., "*African Nations Struggle for Independence*", on [online]. *International Rescue Committee (IRC)*. Available at: https://www.rescue.org/article/african-nations-struggle-independence, 2008.

Saro-Wiwa, K., "The Language of African Literature: A Writer's Testimony", in *Research in African Literatures*, Vol 23, No 1, pp. 153–157, 1992.

Senghor, Leopold S., *Leopold Sedar Senghor: The Collected Poetry*, University of Virginia Press, 1998.

The School of Life, "Africa After Independence", in [online]. *The School of Life*. Available at: https://www.theschooloflife.com/article/africa-after-independence/ (no date).

Vallin, V.M., "France as the Gendarme of Africa, 1960–2014", in *Political Science Quarterly*, Vol 130, No 1, pp. 79–101, 2015.

Vonyó, T., "Post-war Reconstruction and the Golden Age of Economic Growth", in the *European Review of Economic History*, Vol 12, No 2, pp. 221–241, 2008.

Wamagatta, E.N., "African Collaborators and Their Quest for Power in Colonial Kenya: Senior Chief Waruhiu wa Kung'u's Rise from Obscurity to Prominence, 1890-1922", in *The International Journal of African Historical Studies*, Vol 41, No 2, pp. 295–314, 2008.

World Nuclear Association, "History of Nuclear Energy—World Nuclear Association", in [online]. *World Nuclear Association*. Available at: https://www.world-nuclear.org/information-library/current-and-future-generation/outline-history-of-nuclear-energy.aspx, 2020.

Zartman, I.W., "Europe and Africa: Decolonization or Dependency?", in *Foreign Affairs*, Vol 54, No 2, pp. 325–343, 1976.

Zeleza, P.T., "Africa's Struggles for Decolonization: From Achebe to Mandela", in *Research in African Literatures*, Vol 45, No 4, pp. 121–139, 2014.

Chapter 6: An Interdependency Stuck in the Past

Adamu, Abdulrahman and Peter, Abraham, "Comparative Analysis of the African and European Union", in *International Journal of Peace and Conflict Studies*, Vol 3, No 1, 2016.

Biko, Humelo, *The Great African Society*, Johannesburg: Jonathan Ball, 2013.

Buruma, Ian, and Margalit, Avishai, *Occidentalism*, 2004.

Carbone, Maurizio (ed.), *The European Union and Africa*, Manchester University Press, 2015.

Cole, Teju, "The White Industrial Saviour Complex", in *The Atlantic*, 12 March 2012.

Colin, Nicole and Demesmay, Claire (eds.), *The Franco-German Relations Seen from Abroad*, Mannheim: Springer, 2020.

Collier, Paul, *The Bottom Billion*, 2007.

Collier, Paul, *The Plundered Planet*, 2010.

Dror, Yehezkel, "Adjusting the Central Mind of Governments to Adversity", in *International Political Science Review*, Vol 7, No 1, 1986.

Dror, Yehezkel, "Priming Political Leaders for Fateful Choices", in e-Journal *World Academy of Arts and Sciences*, issue 6, February 2015.

Duke, Simon, *The European External Action Service and Public Diplomacy*, The Hague: Clingendael Papers, 2013.

Dussey, Robert, *L'Afrique malade*, Paris: Picollec, 2008.

European Centre for Development Policy Management (ECDPM), *The Future of ACP-EU Relations*, Maastricht, 2016.

European Commission Libraries, www.eucommissionlibraries/africa.

Fannon, Franz, *The Wretched of the Earth*, 1961.

Gbadamassi, Falila, «L'Euraffrique, la fausse rupture de Nicolas Sarkozy», in *Le Nouvel Afrik.Com*, 27.7.2007.

Gill, Graeme and Angosto-Fernandez, Luis, "Symbolism and Politics", in *Politics, Religion and Ideology*, Vol 19, 2012.

Green, Toby, *A Fistful of Shells*, London: Penguin, 2019.

Gretschmann, Klaus, " Politikgestaltung im Spannungsfeld von Nationalstaat und Europäische Union", in *Aus Politik und Zeitgeschichte*, 5, 2001.

Gretschmann, Klaus, "New Challenges for European Governance", in Kakabadse, A., and Schepers, S. (eds.), *Rethinking the Future of Europe*, Palgrave Macmillan, 2014.

Hansen, Peo, and Jonsson, Stefan, *Eurafrica, the Untold History of European Integration and Colonialism*, London: Bloomsbury Academic, 2014.

Heldring, Leander and Robinson, James A., *Colonialism and Economic Development in Africa*, National Bureau of Economic Research, Cambridge (US), Working paper 18566, 2012.

Héraud, Guy, "L'inter-étatique, le supranational et le fédéral", in *Archives du Philosophie du Droit*, Vol 6, 1961.

High Level Group on AU-EU Partnership, Reports 31.1.2020 and 16.9.2020, www.highlevelgroup.eu

High Level Group on EU Governance Innovation, report January 2021, www.highlevelgroup.eu

High Level Group on Innovation Policy, 2016, *Report on Public Sector Reform*, www.highlevelgroup.eu

High Level Group on Trade Policy Innovation, *Report 2019*, www.highlevelgroup.eu

Islam, Shada, "Reforming Migration Requires Tackling EU Pride and Prejudice", in *EuObserver*, 31 August 2022.

Jensen, Lars, *Post-colonial Europe*, Abingdon on Thames: Routledge, 2020.

Kuhn, Thomas, *The Structure of Scientific Revolutions*, Chicago University Press, 1965.

Lehne, Stephan, *Is There Hope for an EU Foreign Policy?*, Carnegie Europe Research Paper, December 2017

Lopes, Carlos, *Africa in Transformation*, Palgrave Macmillan, 2019.

Mandani, Mahmood, "State and Civil Society in Contemporary Africa", in *Africa Development*, Vol 15, No 3–4, CODESRIA 1990.

Mazzucato, Mariana, *The Entrepreneurial State*, Sage, 2011.

Mbeki, Moeletsi, *Architects of Poverty*, Picador, 2009.

Mengisteab, Kidane, *Traditional Institutions of Governance in Africa*, Oxford Research Online, 23 March 2019.

Meredith, Martin, *The State of Africa, A History Since Independence*, Simon & Schuster, 2005.

Michalopoulos, S., and Papaioannou, E., *Historical Legacies and African Development*, in US National Bureau of Economic Research, 2018.

Michalski, Anna, "*The EU as a Soft Power*", in Melissen, Jan, *The New Public Diplomacy*, Palgrave Macmillan, 2005.

Moïsi, Dominique, *The Geo-politics of Emotion*, 2009.

Noseir, Mohammed, "Questioning Western National Moral Values", *in Asia Times*, 28 April 2020.

Nye, Joseph, *Soft power, the Means to Success in World Politics*, UK: Hachette UK, 2009.

Piketty, Thomas, *Une brève histoire de l'égalité*, Paris Ed. du Seuil, 2021.

Piketty, Thomas, *A Brief History of Equality*, Belknap Press, 2022.

Rood, J.Q.T, *Een nieuw Benelux Verdrag, elan voor nieuwe samenwerking*, in SEW Clingendael, No 5, 2010.

Sabel, C., and Zeitlin, J., *Experimentalist Governance in the EU*, Oxford University Press, 2010.

Said, W. Edward, *Orientalism*, Pantheon Books, 1978.

Said, W. Edward, *Culture and Imperialism*, Chatto & Windus, 1993.

Schepers, S., "Collaborative Governance", in Gretschmann, K. and Schepers, S. (eds.), *Revolutionising European Innovation Policy*, London: Palgrave Macmillan, 2016.
Sharkey, H.J. "African Colonial States", in Parker, J. and Reids, R. (eds.), *The Oxford Handbook of Modern African History*, 2013.
Táíwò, Olúfémi, *How Colonialism Pre-Empted Modernity in Africa*, Indian University Press, 2010.
Van de Meersche, Paul, *De Europese Integratie*, Leuven: Davidsfonds, 1971.
van Middelaar, Luuk, *The Passage to Europe*, Yale University Press, 2014.
Zielonka, Jan, "The EU as International Actor, Unique or Ordinary", in *European Foreign Affairs Review*, 16, 2011.

Chapter 7: Facing the Future

Stephan Harry, Power Michael, Hervey Angus Fane and Steenkamp Fonseca Raymond, *The Scramble for Africa in the 21st Century*, Renaissance Press, 2006.
High Level Group on African-European Partnership, report January 2022, www.highlevelgroup.eu
Lopes, Carlos, *Africa in Transformation*, Palgrave Macmillan, 2019.
Nooke, Günther and Kraus, Christiane (eds.), *Cities Not Camps*, 2022.

Index

A
Africa-Europe interaction, 76
African-European interdependencies, 115
African-European Partnership, 144
African-European relationship, 118
African humanism, 69
African kingdoms, viii
African nationalism, 93
African post-colonial independence, 107
African Pre-colonial Social and Political Structures, 67
African societies, 3
African socio-political systems, 88
African Values Systems, 85
Africa's Ancient Economies, 39
Akan states, 21
Aksum, 30
Alaafin, 20
Alliances, 57
Animals, 9
Ashanti-European trade, 21
A Veil of Ignorance, 1

B
Belgian Congo, 23
Benin, 18
Botswana, 27

C
Carthage, 12
Central African Kingdoms, 22
Christianity, 59
Civilisation, 1
Clans to City States, 73
Colonialism, 91
Colonial oppression, 95
Colonisation, 82
Communal kinship, 94
Communitarianism, 69
Constructive Interdependence, 130
Cosmopolitanism, 4
Cowry shells, 51
Crops, 42
Currencies in pre-colonial Africa, 47

D
Dahomey kingdom, 20

E
East African Kingdoms, 29
Economic activities in pre-colonial Africa, 42
Economic decline, 62
Edo people, 18
Egypt and North African Kingdoms, 10
Ethiopia, 6
EU-Africa strategy, 132
Eurocentrism, vii
Europe's golden age, 100
European Economic Community (EEC), 102
European Free Trade Association (EFTA), 102
European imperialism, 2

F
Fish, 42
Fula people, 43

G
Ghana Empire, 15
Gold, 9
Gold mining, 46

I
Ife, 20
Industrialisation, 3
Institutional asymmetries, 151
Iron, 9
Islam, 59
Ivory, 9

K
Kanem-Borno Empire, 18
kingdom of D'mt, 30
Kingdom of Kongo, 22
Kingdom of Rwanda, 34
Kush, 10

L
Leo Apostel, 130
Leo Frobenius, 7
Libyan Desert, 9
Livestock, 42

M
Madagascar, 55
Mali Empire, 15
Mandela, Nelson, 67
Manillas, 52
Mansa Musa, 16
Manufacturing, 44
Mapungubwe, 27
Mediterranean, 9
Mining, 46
Missionary churches, 96

N
Nubia, 10

O
Obsidian, 9
Occidentalism, vii
Omoluabi, 70
Organization of African Unity (OAU), 106
Ottoman, 14
Ottoman Empire, 34
Oyo, 20

P
Partnership strategy, 151
Pharaoh, 11
Political order, 4
Portuguese, 22
Post-colonial African realities, 89
Pre-colonial Africa, 40
Pre-colonial Political Order in Africa, 9

R
Republic of Benin, 20
Roman Empire, 14
Ruling families, 76

S
Sahel, 15
Salt, 9
Scramble for Africa, 23, 91
Senegal, 9
Senghor, Leopold, x
Silver, 9
Slave trade, 20
Social exploitation, 2
Sokoto Caliphate, 18
Songhai, 16
Southern African Kingdoms, 24
Spices, 9
Struggle for independence, 91
Sub-Saharan Africa, 6

T
Timbuktu, 49
Tribalism, 84
Tribalist, 85
Tutu, Desmond, 67

U
Ubuntu, 67
Uganda, 34
United Nations Charter, 68

W
West African Kingdoms, 15
Wheat, 9
World Wars 1 and 2, 99

Z
Zimbabwe, 28
Zulu kingdom, 26

Printed in the United States
by Baker & Taylor Publisher Services